Susan,

Hope you enjoy
learning more about
your vision!

Jay Hurley

PRAISE FOR *The Other Side of Vision*

"As an author and speaker, Dr. Jay Sterling is engaging and a master of metaphorical illustrations. He is the 'go-to-guy' for innovative thinking and endless creativity."

—TOM ANTION
NSA speaker and advisor to thousands of businesses across the globe

"Quite frankly this is the most interesting and thought provoking self-help book I have ever had the pleasure to read. Well done, kudos, and countless accolades. This is a tremendous accomplishment and renews my faith on the power and integrity of self-help books."

—ELLI MAAS DAVIS
Professional writer and author of *The Humours of Folly*

"This is an extraordinary book. Dr. Sterling has written an energizing, transformative, easily accessible book that offers hope, breadth of perspective, and proof that 'there is more than meets the eye.' His ingenious writing style encourages and guides you to achieve true success, not achievement found through conformity, but success born from achieving one's own goals and realizing one's own potential to the fullest. Congratulations to Dr. Sterling."

—JOSEPH MICHELLI, PH.D.
National Best Selling Author of *The Starbucks Experience*

Master How to Perceive More and Achieve More

THE OTHER SIDE OF
VISION

JAY STERLING

Advantage®

Published by Advantage, Charleston, South Carolina.
Member of Advantage Media Group.

ADVANTAGE is a registered trademark and the Advantage colophon is a trademark of Advantage Media Group, Inc.

Printed in the United States of America.

ISBN: 978-1-59932-080-9
LCCN: 2009907703

This publication is designed to provide accurate and authoritative information in regard to the subject matter covered. It is sold with the understanding that the publisher is not engaged in rendering legal, accounting, or other professional services. If legal advice or other expert assistance is required, the services of a competent professional person should be sought.

Most Advantage Media Group titles are available at special quantity discounts for bulk purchases for sales promotions, premiums, fundraising, and educational use. Special versions or book excerpts can also be created to fit specific needs.

For more information, please write: Special Markets, Advantage Media Group, P.O. Box 272, Charleston, SC 29402 or call 1.866.775.1696.

Visit us online at **advantagefamily**.com

PREFACE

When I was approached to write a preface for this book, I was honored as both a friend of Jay and a fellow professional. Then, I stepped back and thought, "Can I simply say this is a must read book?" Or, do I comment on the fact that Jay truly sees the world from a perspective that creative minds envy?

In a town accessible to both city and country lifestyles, there is a sign telling the world that Jay's optometry office serves the community with pride. Years ago, when I first went to his office for an eye examination, I sat waiting for my appointment time and watched the staff in action. Every person was made to feel special. Then, I realized, Jay had mastered the ability to create a team that shared his perspective on his business; this eye doctor who was about to examine my eyes gave his employees the gift of "perfect vision."

Perfect Vision is not something that eyeglasses can provide. Perfect Vision is a state of mind; a way of seeing the world with the end goal in sight.

Jay was clearly walking his own walk. He not only knew the value of keeping your goals in perspective, but he understood the value of seeing the world from the perspective required at any moment. Each patient was a unique individual requiring that they be treated from a different perspective. From business people to children to patients with special needs, his staff changed their perspectives fluidly.

Suddenly an irony occurred when this man who understood the need to see the world in unique and different ways diligently worked with me to give me ocular clarity.

I had known Jay for many years before the above interaction, but it was on this day that I first learned to appreciate the exquisite manner in which he melded his worlds together. I had always known him to be a successful businessman, a world-renowned illusionist, and always respected his ability to speak on the platform, but on this day, I recognized the balance that he had achieved in his life; I saw the common thread that was the root of his success: He knew the value of seeing the world not as it is or how it should be, but how he *wanted* it to be.

In these pages, you will share Jay's unique perspectives of the world in which we live, and as you read his thoughts, you will acquire the tools to see the world from a perspective that will lead you to your own personal level of clarity and "Perfect Vision."

—Joseph A. Curcillo, III, Esquire

TABLE OF CONTENTS

INTRODUCTION

Much of society appears to be on an endless journey, in search of "the ultimate new": the newest, the biggest, the latest, and the greatest. In reality, rather than searching for new landscapes, it may be more beneficial to simply have new eyes. This book offers simple tools and strategies for use in a complex world to encourage and enhance our own imaginations.

Everything that we have in our lives began with someone's imagination. Most of us accept our visual function just as it is, but much of what we see is actually distorted. Think of Thomas Edison, or Albert Einstein, or Pablo Picasso. Their ability to see the world began with the same physiological eye structure that we have, yet they had a much greater capacity to stretch their imaginations and see "common things" differently.

The continual changes of life offer an endless source of opportunities. The key is to be able to "see" them.

Our eyes gather information and interpret our world for us quite effortlessly, and in a more sophisticated way than the most expensive computers on the planet. We take most of our visual knowledge for granted, rather than tap into its full potential. Once we better understand how our visual knowledge is deceiving us, we can gain new perspectives about what "we believe" we're seeing. Much of our future success will be based on our ability to alter these interpretations and be creative. First we have to respect and appreciate our innate capacity to do this.

Life is not about finding yourself; it's about creating yourself.

There are times when our creativity is automatic. We use it instinctively to make a memorable impression when meeting a new acquaintance or to improvise and accommodate a comfortable lifestyle for our family. Creativity is also essential for modern day communication and aids greatly in speeding up our learning process. The laws of today's work environment have established that just one mistake can jeopardize our job security. On the other hand, it may necessitate only one outstanding idea for us to control our destiny and even retire wealthy.

So how do we become more creative? As children we instinctively ask "why" everything is the way it is… why, why, why? We are naturally curious and aren't afraid to ask questions. There is an inborn passion for understanding everything around us until our parents become frustrated answering our obscure queries, and simply reply, "Because I said so." Or, "That's just the way it is." Unfortunately, this also starts the process of diminishing our inborn quest for limitless possibilities.

This book first demonstrates, surprisingly, how often our eyes are deceived on an everyday basis. Secondly, it shows how simply our perception can be improved, using fun techniques that can be easily implemented. And lastly, it reveals how these ideas can be naturally incorporated into everyday life. Almost instantly you will broaden the way you see and heighten your awareness of new perspectives.

Some of these concepts may seem common place while others are much more abstract. If you're already familiar with a few of them, you know their value. The ability to use your eyes creatively is already inside of you. My goal is to give you the leverage needed for developing these ideas so that they become second nature and then multiply synergistically.

READER BEWARE

Advisory

Our approach to life in much of what we do is far too methodical. If we ever hope to become more attentive, perceptive, creative, imaginative, and inventive we can't continue to think the same way we have in the past.

In that light, you are encouraged to *not* read this book page for page, in numerical order, from start to finish. Each of us differs drastically in the way we learn. Living should not be about limiting our curiosity, our excitement, and our thirst for the unknown. Allow your heart, mind, and emotions to take their own course.

It's quite possible to learn and experience something utterly different when reading the exact same paragraph at another time and place. Hopefully, these pages will continue to offer you a wide array of extraordinary thoughts depending upon when and what you choose to read... enjoy your open mind.

The most beautiful thing we can experience is the mysterious. It is the source of all true art and science. He to whom this emotion is a stranger, who can no longer pause to wonder and stand rapt in awe, is as good as dead: his eyes are closed. —Albert Einstein

---

SECTION 1:
PERCEPTUAL
REALITY
(DISCOVERY)

IT'S NOT WHAT YOU SEE—

IT'S WHAT YOU *THINK* YOU SEE.

CHAPTER ONE

DON'T BLINK

⓵

Picture This

All we need to do is close our eyes for thirty seconds on a busy street corner, and we are instantly reminded of how challenged we would be without our ability to see.

All five of our senses help to create our reality. But our vision, our perception, is responsible for at least eighty-three percent of our sensory information. Not only do we think in terms of pictures, but everything we do is actually understood through mental images.

In other words, when we see the word "apple," we don't say in our mind the letters a-p-p-l-e. Instead, we imagine what an apple looks like. If we're told that someone is wealthy, we generally don't picture their bank statement or what stock shares they own. We picture a yacht, a private jet, or a massive estate. We imagine a lifestyle typical of the rich and famous.

There was a time when the only source of communication was oral. Now we communicate with pictures and have become primarily dependent on them even more than words. Today, by far, the majority of our communication is visual, which offers the quickest means to disseminate the maximum amount of information. As we watch current-day movies, sports, and advertising we find more quick cuts and editing within a ten second span than ever before. And even the signage we see has become more image-oriented.

Years ago a sign would read "No Cell Phones Allowed." Or in an attempt to appear friendlier, it might read, "Thank You For Not Using Your Cell Phone." Now we simply use a sign with a red line through a picture of a cell phone. Using a split second glance, we interpret the same information in a fraction of the time—in any country it's displayed, without a language barrier.

A recent article in *Wired* magazine emphasized corporate America's awareness of this. Rather than forwarding the typical "written" office memos to its workforce, larger companies (from Microsoft to Wal-Mart) recognize the time saving capability of sending an uncomplicated picture or series of pictures to relay an important message. Instead of having employees read about the details of an upcoming meeting and who is required to attend, they might draw a simplistic picture or even a cartoon rendition of the company boardroom. A wall clock in the diagram displays the starting time. Photo-name tags reveal who is expected to be present. And pictures on the table preview the topics for discussion.

We can obviously interpret the concept of a picture much more rapidly than a lengthy paragraph of words. Since these words are ultimately used to create a mental picture anyway, we are essentially eliminating the most time consuming step to the cognitive process. Most of our lives, from business to entertainment, are dependent on visual communication. Although we never really see what we think we see.

We would like to believe that what we (think we) see is the actual world in front of us. But the retina of our eye can't duplicate an exact copy of what we look at. In fact, nothing could be further from the truth. When light enters through the pupil, more than a million nerve fibers in the optic nerve must translate and transmit electrical impulses to the brain. For us to see properly three things must happen simultaneously: first the light from the image we are looking at must be reduced in size to fit inside our pupil, then all of this scattered light must be bent to match the inside curvature of our eye, and thirdly this resulting image must accurately imprint across the entire retinal surface. So... how does that make what we think we see different?

Our eyes have the distinct ability to look at a flat picture and interpret it as being three-dimensional. They will also intentionally distort the size of an object to make it more understandable. This means our vision is nowhere near an exact replica of what we see. And, surprisingly, this process is automatic, happening long before our mind even becomes involved in the perceptual process.

Our vision rules our perception, and our perception becomes our reality.

From the time we first awaken, our perception is already attempting to create a more realistic interpretation of the flat picture in front of us. For instance, usually the very first thing we do in the morning is look at ourselves in the mirror (which can, visually, be the scariest part of our day). Unknowingly, our eyes have already doubled the size of what they see.

If you don't believe this, take a moment to place a ruler flat against your bathroom mirror and measure the vertical dimension of the reflection of your face. You will find that it measures approximately four and a half inches high in the mirror. In reality the actual size of your face is closer to nine inches high.

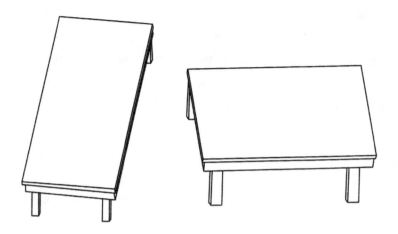

In much the same way, the picture above created by Roger Shepard shows two tabletops that appear to be completely different sizes. Yet using a ruler, again, you'll find them to be exactly the same. Even after proving this to yourself your eyes refuse to accept it.

Our eyes repeatedly see something other than our true reality. But this can also be the impetus for the origination of many new ideas. Have you ever wondered what an unfamiliar object was used for, and only after discovering its intended use, realized that your initial *guess* might have applications, too? Well, that is indeed a very valid and viable strategy in the process of how many things are invented.

Sight Unseen

Our perception, unlike our sight, is a learned process. It is both consciously and unconsciously learned. It can be studied and improved upon as a true educational skill. Our perception typically improves with age due to our education, life experiences, and preconceived notions.

Quite unknowingly we mentally fabricate many illusions on a daily basis. These self-constructed deceptions cause us to become overly accepting of what we think we see, leading us to an innocent complacency. As these ongoing patterns continue to dominate our visual understanding, we eventually become trapped, expecting to see certain things that may not even exist.

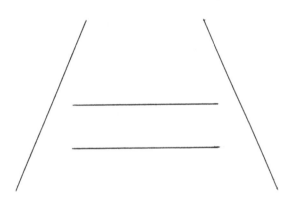

In the picture above, a quick glance seems to reveal that the top horizontal line is longer than the lower one, even though they are exactly the same size. This well-known Ponzo illusion deceives us because the upper line is influenced by the surrounding slanted lines, which create an artificial depth. From our previous experiences of seeing a road narrow in the distance, we feel the upper line should be proportionately shorter, which creates the illusion of it being longer.

We like to think of ourselves as being very observant. But our mind bases the majority of its interpretations of what we see on generalizations and patterns that are most familiar to us. Our perception anticipates what might be most probable and easiest to interpret before looking at something in more detail. Over time this process becomes even more hard wired. We make more and more assumptions as our visual attentiveness declines.

For example, imagine walking through a room at work or at home that you frequent multiple times a day. If one of the pictures hanging on the wall is replaced with another, using the same original frame, the replacement picture may go completely unnoticed, possibly for weeks, since our vision instinctively searches for differences that are more profound. This is so similar to the original pattern of the room that our eyes assume there is too little change to warrant our attention.

In another instance, we may walk into a familiar room that has been freshly painted, even a moderately different color, yet our eyes are more drawn to the clutter on the floor or a chair that's been moved. We can become so preoccupied that the crisp new walls are totally unobserved. Have you ever been on a familiar road and caught yourself saying, "I don't remember that building... I wonder how long it's been there?"

Over time these visual expectations can even spill over into other aspects of our day as our lives fall into patterns of systematic routines. We will often anticipate how a certain situation will appear well before we actually see it. One factor behind this is that our vision is dependent on our eyes making many continuous assumptions about what they see. They are constantly scanning the broadest view possible, with far too many details to digest all at once. Even though this leads to an inaccurate picture, it's a necessary process for us to function and navigate through life. Our brain gathers every tidbit of information it receives from our sight to determine what is most relevant for us to comprehend.

The eye can create an image, but only the mind can determine what is real.

It would be impossible to drive, play a sport, or engage in most forms of entertainment if it required breaking down every minute detail of all the things taking place in front of us at any given moment. Through experience and repetition, our perception improves, as we rely on our preconceived notions and previous experiences to automatically evaluate what we see and help us make quicker decisions. This is what creates our reality.

As we glance at the picture of the glass on the next page, the olive appears to be sinking into the bottom half of the drink. But taking a moment to measure where it's actually located we find that it's exactly in the center, much different than our first impression. Again, this is just the way our eyes attempt to evaluate linear forms. As we make mistakes in our judgment, our brain extrapolates what it learns so that better choices can be made in the future.

In the same way, when we look at a three-dimensional cube, we unknowingly disregard that we can only ever see three sides of the cube at once. We can never see a fourth, fifth, or sixth side at the same time. No matter how we rotate any object, our eyes can only see half of it at any given moment. Our brain has the continual task of creating a visual impression for us to imagine, which allows us to assume what is on the other side.

This is very similar to the process that takes place when we watch a movie or a video. Movies really consist of many individual pictures passing in front of the eye in rapid sequence. As the eyes gather information from this altering source of light, our mind creates the sensation of life-like animation. When viewing single frames separately, or seeing them out of order, our vision can no longer grasp the essence of what the video represents in its entirety.

If we look at the first three lines on the next page, our perception begins searching for a relevant pattern. It's not quite certain about their significance since there doesn't appear to be any logical meaning for their arrangement. When we make a minor change to the third line, as in the second figure, our vision eventually concludes that the lines

23

represent a shadow, and we finally recognize the common configuration. Can you see the edges of the letter they form? We are ultimately dependent on trusting our perception to create our own perspective of reality.

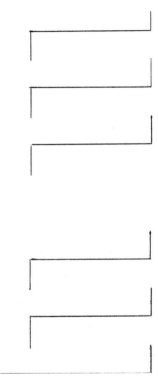

An illusionist can take full advantage of this, knowing how our eyes resolve what they see and how our mind formulates its own perception. A magical obscurity doesn't take place in the space in front of us as much as the space inside our head. One primary purpose of performing an illusion is to encourage an audience to question "what if... this were possible." An instrumental difference between the average person and one who is more inventive is that the latter one makes a habit of questioning "everything" that the eyes supposedly see.

Mesmer - Eyes

Whenever we attempt to focus on one specific object, say a word on this page, we trust that our eyes are compliant and see only one thing, too. Because we can't feel the constant movement of our eyes, we are unaware that they are in an endless state of motion, much like bees around a hive. Darting haphazardly in all directions, (these movements are known as saccades), our eyes are continually scanning as they attempt to assess everything around us. Our primary focal point is a very small entity of our entire field of view. While our extent of side vision can be helpful, our area of optimal vision is much smaller than we realize.

Use the tips of your thumb and forefinger to create a circle and extend your hand to arm's length. Looking through this hole gives a very close approximation to the size of our clearest vision. The area inside our eye that corresponds to this is called the fovea. It is less than two millimeters wide and the only portion of the retina (the area at the back of the eye responsible for seeing) available for optimal clarity, which is what we refer to as 20/20 vision. This is because the fovea has the largest number of photoreceptors, which the brain requires for converting light into a picture. Our eyes can never see an entire picture clearly at any given moment.

Look closely into a mirror at the reflection of your right eye. Now quickly change your focus to your left eye. As often as you do this, you will find it impossible to see your eyes move. This is because our eyes can only see at the endpoints of their movements. Our brain suppresses the blurred images during the saccadic movements, and while it does this we are briefly blind. Even though these individual movements last only a fraction of a second (approximately 75 to 150 milliseconds), the additive effect is that we have no visual function for almost an hour each day.

Our mind has the task of gathering many individual glimpses from our somewhat limited sight to artificially create a picture. It can be quite different than what is actually present in front of us. This process can be likened to a professional photo shoot. Imagine a super-model striking dozens of poses in very short duration. The camera keeps clicking away, almost every second, as she moves from one position to the next. Our fovea, which lies at the center of the retina, and is also thought of as the sharpest part of the "film" in the back of our eye, works in much the same way. With each brief snapshot from our constant eye movement it must now analyze a new and different picture. All the while our brain must systematically meld each of these pictures together to create our presumed reality. This one small area of the retina is the only part ever in perfect focus at any given time, and only during the very brief moment when our eyes stop their continual movement to change direction.

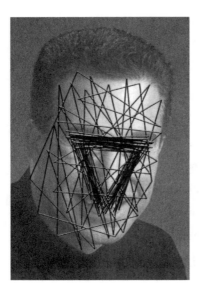

The picture here shows a typical example of how the eyes scan across a person's face in chaotic fashion to create a complete picture. They continually return to the eyes and mouth, as each of these are primary focal points. In between, they dart all over while gathering information, but they can only make sense of something when they stop. The additive effects of each of those stopping points are what create our vision... an interpretation of our perceived reality.

If, for instance, we are trying to read a sign down the road, only one tiny aspect of our eye, the fovea, lines up perfectly with the sign. The point of reference on the sign is referred to as our fixation point or line of sight. The rest of the sign is seen as being slightly blurred, but with the use of our constant eye motion and peripheral vision, our brain can make sense of what we're trying to see.

I am reminded of a time when I was standing on a mosaic in an ancient cathedral. We might first become aware of the countless number of small individual tiles so strategically placed to create such a masterful relic. To look closely at these, one piece at a time, might reveal that many of them are comprised of just a single color. It is only when we stand back for a composite view that we begin to appreciate the artistic value of the complete picture.

Anytime we look at a television screen or a printed photograph, which are also comprised of thousands of digitally created dots of color, the same perceptual process occurs.

It's difficult to see the picture when you're inside the frame.

Being too close to a problem or narrowing our focus too intently can keep us from seeing the broader picture and often the obvious answer. As a society that becomes excited about ever tinier gadgets that continue to carry even greater amounts of information, we have to remind ourselves that sometimes smaller and closer don't always offer the best opportunity to perceive.

Do you see the inherent values in both getting closer and farther away from many other aspects of what we see? Each one of these can dramatically change our perception, as well as refine and redirect the way we think.

Partially Blind

One of the most intricate and complex structures in the world is integrated into the back of our eyes. It is known as the optic nerve and is responsible for delivering information from the retina to the brain. This optic nerve creates an actual blind spot in each of our eyes because there are no photoreceptors where it attaches, and therefore, no functioning retina or vision.

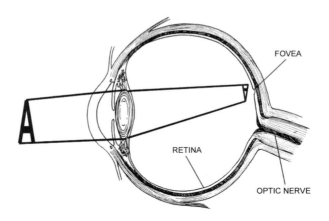

Try covering one eye with your hand and then extending your other arm and forefinger as you point to an object across the room. Line your finger up so that it's right on top of your target. Now, while still watching the target, slowly move your finger in a horizontal plane away from center. (If you're using your right eye and right finger, slowly move your finger toward the right side of the room.) You will find a point where the tip of your finger gradually fades out of focus and then comes back into focus again. This is the actual blind spot for that eye.

This is one of the advantages of having two eyes. Each eye helps to make up for the blind spot of the other, so the blind spots essentially go unnoticed. When we want to remove a blemish or an abstract mark from a photograph, say for a magazine cover, we can digitally correct it with a software program (such as Photoshop). It searches and makes use of the surrounding colors to mask and camouflage the erroneous mark we want to delete. Our eyes work in tandem to do the same thing. Each eye can individually compensate for its own blind spot, too, based on what the expected picture should look like and the colors and shadows surrounding it.

There is another instance when we are not using both eyes equally. Notice when you look far enough to your left or right, your nose begins to interfere with the view of one eye. At that point our eyes are no longer working together as a team, and we lose the majority of our depth perception, also known as stereopsis. This is also when more of our peripheral vision must come into play, even though it has less photoreceptors and our vision isn't nearly as accurate.

Although our peripheral vision spans almost one hundred and eighty degrees, this diminishes drastically when our bodies are in motion. When driving a car at sixty miles per hour our peripheral vision shrinks to less than forty-five degrees, or approximately one fourth of what it would be when we are still. This compromises our vision so severely that it makes a strong case for the need to be extremely alert and minimize our distractions while driving.

Another phenomenon we deal with is that while we may think we are using each of our eyes equally, most people have one eye that is more dominant. When we use a camera's viewfinder or a monocular microscope, for example, only one eye can be used to focus while the other eye automatically suppresses what it sees. We rely on our capability of doing this so that our vision doesn't become confused. If one eye is not suppressed, our brain has the challenge of trying to make sense of two entirely different view points at the same time, which it cannot do.

You can demonstrate this to yourself by, again, extending your arm and pointing to a specific object across the room. Now alternately cover each of your eyes with your other hand. You will notice that one of yours eyes will always be lined up with the object you're focusing on and the other will not. The one that appears to be off centered from your focus is intentionally being suppressed. The other eye is your dominant one.

Some individuals have a permanent suppression in one eye known as amblyopia. This occurs when one eye didn't receive the necessary exposure to high resolution acuity before the age of seven or eight. This can be due to the eye muscles not functioning properly, in that the eyes are not aligned together as a team. It can also occur because of a disproportionate clarity between the eyes, which would have required corrective lenses at a young age. After that time period of seven or eight years (which will vary from person to person), the vision in that particular eye will never improve beyond the best acuity it has previously experienced.

Astigmatism is another visual anomaly that many people have and a factor that commonly distorts our ability to see clearly. If you require an astigmatic correction, try removing your glasses (or contact lenses) for a moment. Now look at the next diagram (you can hold it closer or further away, as necessary, to help see it clearer) and you will discover that some of the spokes of the wheel are much more in focus than the ones ninety degrees away. More people have astigmatism than not, although it can easily be corrected with prescription lenses.

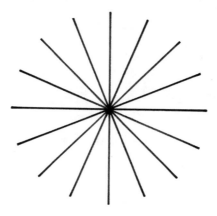

Our eyes are designed so that we are able to focus on only one plane at a time. When someone has astigmatism, their eyes are compromised in that they can see limited parts of multiple planes. Because this is very confusing it results in a generalized blur. With corrected vision we can see clearly at three feet or twenty feet, but cannot see both at once. If we focus on a near image the far image is blurred. And conversely, if we focus on a far image the near one is blurred. Because the real world is comprised of an infinite number of focal distances, much of what we believe we're seeing is essentially out of focus.

This attribute normally works to our benefit in allowing us to concentrate on the center of our attention. Otherwise, we would be constantly battling an endless array of distractions. Knowing this, how can we use it to our advantage for expanding the way we think? What do you notice when you don't allow your focus to remain on any specific plane, changing the distance of your focus at least every five seconds?

Too Close to See

Since much of today's lifestyle revolves around the use of a computer, handheld electronic devices, or some form of "close up" reading, we are steadily taking steps toward becoming a near point society. An ever-growing portion of both our work and entertainment now occurs within arm's length. Both as adults and children we are on computers a sizeable portion of the day. We have become incessantly dependent on our Blackberries, iPods, and GPS systems. Many children become obsessed with a variety of handheld electronic games before they ever enter school. The result of this constant strain on our eyes is that society now has an exceptionally higher incidence of myopia, which is another term for nearsightedness.

Some people are predestined to become nearsighted because of their family history. Others may develop it due to the physiological shape of their eyes. In this case, the internal structures of the eyes don't project the image they are viewing far enough to reach the retina. Most often in today's world it's because of the excess amount of close work we do.

Our eyes are in their most relaxed state when we are focusing on something between the distances of twenty feet and as far as we can see. However, when we look at something much closer, say only five feet away, ironically our eyes are working much harder. As a child, I naturally assumed that the closer I would hold something to my eyes, the easier it would be to see. Nothing could be further from the truth. In fact, the strain required for our eyes to focus very closely is somewhat disproportionate to what we might expect.

Let's say that you're reading a book at a distance of twenty-four inches, and you decide to move it closer, to only twelve inches away. Moving it half way closer means that your eyes now have to work approximately four times harder in order to adjust their focus and see the book clearly. If you move the book half way closer again, to six inches away, it's now roughly sixteen times harder on your eyes... essentially an exponential increase.

Since this eyestrain is so subtle, it's extremely difficult for us to notice and understand because we don't "feel" it. It's doesn't seem like hard work for us. To better illustrate, if you were to hold your arm out horizontally from your shoulder, it would be quite easy to hold it in that position for a short period of time. But if you attempted to keep it there for even ten minutes, it would become extremely tiresome.

This same principle applies with our ability to focus. Because our eyes have a much stronger capacity than necessary to compensate for our needs, we are often unaware of the underlying strain and tiredness that exist. We are readily distracted by the task at hand.

In another comparison, if we were to maintain a structured work out schedule and repeatedly lift heavy weights, our muscles would naturally grow and enlarge in an effort to accommodate their anticipated demands. A similar change takes place when we strain our focusing ability day after day. When we do excessive amounts of close work, our eyes also try to accommodate our demands. After continually focusing at a very close range, for hours at a time, month after month, our eyes become fatigued and permanently adjusted to the working distance that is most often required of them. We then gradually become more nearsighted as our eyes begin resisting their ability to relax to a more distant focal point.

While in one instance our eyes try to acclimate to our needs, they can also be very selective in what they see, sometimes seemingly beyond our control. A great example can be found on YouTube as you watch "Gorilla in Our Midst." In fact, you'll enjoy it much more if you take a moment to look at it now, before you continue reading, otherwise the paragraph below will ruin a wonderful surprise. Go ahead... I'll wait for you.

Hopefully you enjoyed the experience of actually witnessing this for yourself. This video was produced by Christopher Chabris from Harvard University and Daniel Simons from the University of Illinois. In the event that you didn't watch it first, the video clip displays two basketball teams, dressed in black and white jerseys, as they pass a basketball back and forth among themselves. The challenge is for you is to count how many passes are made during the short clip. Ironically, we become so focused on counting the number of passes to be sure we get the correct answer that most of us don't notice someone dressed in a large gorilla suit walking right through the middle of the players. The gorilla even stops to look right into the camera before dancing off again. More than fifty percent of the viewers entirely miss seeing the gorilla until they watch it for the second or third time.

It's amazing that our eyes can become so riveted on one object they fail to see another more unusual one right in front of us, especially since the gorilla is ten times larger that the basketball. It's exceptionally difficult to concentrate our attention on more than one area at a time.

Our eyes can be either naturally or intentionally drawn to whatever catches our attention, and they cannot see two things at once. We often have to correct our focus to what we intentionally want to perceive. Below is the famous picture of a woman that dates back to a German postcard more than two hundred years ago. Can you see her? Actually there are two different women within the same illustration, depending on where your eyes choose to focus. Neither viewpoint is more correct that the other, but our eyes can never see both of them simultaneously. It's just that our eyes are selective, based on cognitive patterns and our previous experiences. So what might we be missing from having only one perspective, possibly never appreciating that there is another point of view?

Pay attention to where you are placing your focus and how it has to change in allowing you to perceive both images. Is it possible to apply the same mechanics for viewing alternative perspectives in other aspects of your environment? You may have to modify your body positioning or even move to another location to appreciate a fresh point of view. At times it may require nothing more than discovering a new way to look at what was always there. Do you look at a room differently before someone important is going to visit?

Ocular Regeneration

Another complicating affect is that our range of focus deteriorates with age. By the time we hit forty or fifty most people become aware of a condition known as Presbyopia, as they now require bifocals. Many people assume that when we reach a certain age they become cursed with the loss of close vision. In actuality, this deterioration is an on-going process that essentially starts at birth.

An infant's world is predominantly very close to him, and he has no problem focusing within inches all day long. As we age, our comfortable near vision range recedes slightly, gradually pushing our ability to focus further away. Suddenly we reach an age when it seems as though our arms aren't long enough to hold anything at the right distance to see it clearly. It may sometimes appear as though this happened over night, but it's actually a very gradual process.

Likewise, with age, we tend to lose our initiative for recognizable accomplishments. Our focus on reaching for our dreams may not be as pronounced as it once was. And our perception of what is even possible may become distorted, too.

Life is a room full of doors... that close over time.

I enjoy running as a way to help me cross-train for other sports that I'm even more passionate about. Several years ago I rolled my foot and twisted my ankle during a run because I stepped into an unapparent hole in the grass. My ankle swelled profusely, and I could barely walk for days. It ruined my workouts for quite some time, and it was several months before I fully recuperated.

I could have decided that because of my injury it would be safer to discontinue training so aggressively. Instead, I subconsciously learned to let my entire body roll with my ankle whenever I unintentionally place it on an uneven surface. Now, as if my brain has a default mode for potential pain, it's become almost instinctual for my whole body to soften, collapse, and roll as a mechanism for self-protection. (This is comparable to the neuro-muscular memory of balance we possess for riding a bike, even though we may not have ridden one in years.) Because my mind still likes to occasionally wander as I run, this automatic memory has saved my ankles on more than one occasion.

Our vision, and in particular, the way in which we focus, can also be trained to meet our specific needs. In our younger years, we tend to explore life the best way we know how, which is very unmethodical. Later, as adults, with our exposure to endless trials and errors, we willingly accept that our ability to compartmentalize creates more efficiency. In this mode, we subconsciously tend to narrow and categorize our focus, too... so it can be equally efficient.

Here's a cautionary note: recognize that there are times when it's genuinely beneficial for our minds to wander aimlessly, especially when trying to tap into our creative juices. The next time you find yourself caught up in a repetitive exercise or a mundane task, try letting go and giving your eyes the chance to visit new and unfamiliar places. You may open a door that you never even knew existed.

CHAPTER TWO

PERCEPTION DECEPTION

Multi-Focal

M any of us can relate to the scenario of inattentive driving while we find ourselves thinking ahead about what we need to do when we reach our destination. Then before we know it, we passed our exit. It has certainly happened to me more than once, as I'm sure it has to many people. It's quite easy to become lost in thought as our subliminal ability to drive goes on autopilot. Our vision can be distracted in many ways, too.

Picture the top of a balance beam, a mere four inches wide and several feet off the floor. Then think of the Olympic athletes who can do flips and back handsprings almost effortlessly, as they land on this surface with little margin for error. Now imagine that I laid a standard two-inch by four-inch piece of lumber across the floor, representing the same width as the balance beam but now at ground level. It would now be rather easy for you or me to walk across it without much of a challenge. In fact, many of us could almost do it blindfolded.

But let's make it even easier. If you picture a board that's eight inches wide, you would have no hesitation at all in walking across it.

Let's say we used one that is sixteen inches wide and still on the floor. You would most likely be willing to skip across it or even do somersaults on top of it without hesitation.

Now, let's replace that same sixteen-inch plank with a sixteen-inch steel beam. Then imagine spanning it from rooftop to rooftop between two ninety-story buildings. If asked to walk across it now, you may feel your blood pressure start to rise as you develop an immense change of heart. Instead of focusing on the beam, your focus instinctually looks beyond its edges to the seemingly endless depth below. Instantly your perception becomes challenged by not focusing where you want it to. Your vision is greatly distracted from the very place you want to look.

The center squares in the diagrams below look much different in size, yet if you measure them you will find them to be absolutely identical. This is because we are so easily influenced by the size of the surrounding squares.

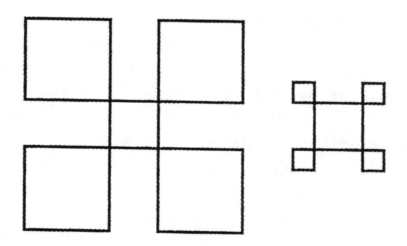

Our ability to focus on the important rather than the distracting is an invaluable skill. Being distracted is the reason for many common failures, including the demise of the most famous ship ever built: the Titanic. Being such an unrivaled and extravagant vessel, all the focus had been placed on the exotic woods, grand chandeliers, and endless amenities— the lavish extras that were deemed so vital to place it in a category of its own. Quite ironically, it was later discovered that the primary reason the Titanic sunk was due to the most understated and least observed parts of this enormous ship.

Undersea explorers found that many of the rivets that held the hull together were imperfect. The smelting process used to make the rivets hadn't eliminated all of the impurities, which made them weak. Any amount of enduring stress would allow them to snap and break more readily than their counterparts no matter how sturdily the rest of it was built. In essence, one of the most essential aspects of the ship received the least amount of focus. Everyone was concerned about how stately and impressionable it would be while ignoring one of its least expensive parts.

When we teach a child how to ride a bike, we tell them not to hit the tree. By saying that, we place part of the focus on the tree. Unexpectedly, they are now more likely to hit it. On the contrary, if we tell them to go around the tree, the child will automatically place their focus on the goal and not the object in their path.

The same priority holds with NASCAR racing. One of the most common phrases among drivers is "don't look where you don't want to go." It's for this reason that they are successful and seldom hit other drivers. They have to steadily maintain their focus on the clear path in front of them, as opposed to the many distracting objects in their periphery.

You can't depend on your eyes when your imagination is out of focus. —Mark Twain

An experiment was once conducted with a newspaper in which a hundred people were offered a chance to win fifty dollars if they could find a particular word written within the copy. A small depiction of the printed word was displayed while encouraging the participants that this may require a very detailed search. As each of them meticulously scrutinized every page, no one ever noticed that in the center of one page was a large advertisement advising that they could receive a hundred dollars by reporting this to those conducting the experiment. Just like the YouTube video mentioned earlier, over concentrating can also narrow our windows of opportunity by limiting our focus to one form of reference.

Think of the last three people you spoke with in person. Can you recall the color of their eyes? During any live conversation, our vision is drawn more to the eyes of another individual than any other distinguishing feature. (Remember the earlier photograph?) It's the way we can best connect with someone and demonstrate our sincerity of engagement. Yet because our eyes work in generalizations, we can seldom remember the color of a person's eyes even though we were just talking to them a moment ago.

It's impossible for our eyes to pinpoint their focus for any length of time, even though this does enhance our peripheral awareness. But a dilemma arises in that our minds have to be selective about all the information we receive at once. Consequently we face a never ending battle of where to place our focus... and how to keep it there.

In the same way that radar and infra red technology will scan and lock onto a particular object, our eyes can essentially mimic these devices as they search for new information. Can you propose any ideas for how this could be used to our advantage? Our quandary is usually not in finding a visual target, but in ignoring its outlying distractions.

Visual Therapy

Because perception is a learned skill, it can either be improved upon through practice and experience or by an alternative methodology known as visual training. As mentioned earlier, our eyes cannot focus at a distance while looking at something close up, and vice versa. Just like a camera, our eyes can only focus on one plane at any given moment. Through the process of visual training, which is a series of simple eye exercises customized for each individual patient, we can learn to change our focus more rapidly and accurately.

While doing my understudy graduate work with Drs. Donald Getz & Gary Etting in Los Angeles, both foremost in their field of behavioral optometry, I found that professional athletes were among the most appreciative patients when treating visual defects. Our responsibility was not only in helping them to attain optimal acuity, but in taking their focusing skills to a higher level. When you can improve a player's batting average from a two hundred to a three hundred, he not only becomes a more valuable player, but is equally rewarded monetarily.

A basic example of an effective exercise for enhancing these focusing skills makes use of a small piece of clear Lucite. By placing a small letter onto the center of the clear material, you can now extend your hand and align it on top of a more distant letter, such as a sign across the street. Now take turns seeing how quickly you can "clearly" focus from one target to the other. This aspect of our focus can be substantially improved with continual practice.

Visual training can also be beneficial for enhancing depth perception, reading skills, and eye-hand coordination. While it's most often reserved for patients with dyslexia and learning challenges, it actually has benefits for anyone. For instance, the value of improving someone's peripheral vision has significant implications when we consider a pilot wanting fewer mistakes while landing or a professional basketball player seeking fewer stolen balls.

While vision is our primary source of sensory information, our hearing is also well integrated into our perceptual behavior. Not long ago a man who was barely noticeable began playing his violin in a Metro station of Washington, D.C. during rush hour. Thousands of people rushed passed him without ever looking in his direction, let alone taking a moment to appreciate his music. He had decided to play several pieces by Bach, but after nearly an hour only six individuals even paused long enough to acknowledge his presence. During that entire time he collected a measly thirty-two dollars with no sign of positive recognition... not even a single clap.

This demonstrates how much we've lost touch with allowing our senses to be in the moment as the man who was playing was Joshua Bell, one of the best musicians of our time. He was playing extremely difficult pieces on an instrument worth well over three million dollars. Had you been in his sold out audience in Boston two days earlier you would have paid an average of a hundred dollars for a ticket to see him perform.

If we are so caught up in the frenzy of our own schedules that we can't stop to appreciate one of the greatest musicians in the world, it stands to reason that our eyes are unquestionably missing much more than we realize. How can we hope to be creative, which means finding the extraordinary in the ordinary, if we don't improve our ability to recognize the obvious? Unless we stop to appreciate life as though looking through the eyes of a child, its complexity can swallow us and disguise its greatest offerings and possibilities.

Before you continue reading, take a moment to look around where you are and try to notice something... anything... that is hidden within simplicity. This is the first step toward allowing your mind the openness to be more creative.

Need for Speed

We have all experienced a cell phone or pager going off when least expected, instantly diverting our attention from anything we were doing. An overdose of electronic interaction can take control of our lives, making it impossible to exist without our Blackberry or laptop. We become so preoccupied with searching, surfing, blogging, and tweeting, while copying, sharing, forwarding, and deleting that there's less and less time to use our eyes effectively. Most conversations don't exist very long before someone has to apologize for checking a text message, receiving a quick call, or thumb typing an answer, all while trying to stay engaged with the other person. Sometimes being connected offers the paradox of too much information and a handicap that rivals not having it at all.

From work to social life to entertainment, our electronic gadgets play a monstrous role in how we navigate through our day. We continue to advance from wires to fiber optics to airwaves in a world where everyone demands to be interconnected. Our memory devices cling onto an ever-growing number of virtual addresses and personal information as we rely on the masses for the majority of our information, education, and recreation... mostly through cyberspace.

The time spent in front of all our media screens is ever increasing as the true outside world competes for the leftover minutes. The balance between our quest for staying informed versus experiencing life in the moment compounds our choices as we look for significance in what we're actually trying to accomplish.

A concern about these uncontrollable and accelerating shifts within our society has garnered so much attention from social scientists that its research has been given a name... "Memetics." Memes, the basic unit of these invisible viruses that continue to spread and infect our culture, have become so pronounced that they now dominate the way we think and live. None of us likes to come to terms with the fact that we may be wrong, especially having to admit that many of our thought patterns are no longer our own.

During the ever hectic pace of each day our attention span becomes increasingly selective in its search for variety and entertainment. The advertising industry and the people behind our many forms of media understand this all too well. They're encouraged by the populace to create the swift edit cuts that we're accustomed to seeing on television and video. We are forever being conditioned to evaluate and digest what we see more rapidly. In turn, this gears us toward making hastened decisions and expecting immediate satisfaction.

Virtual conversations now require added layers of attention as they attempt to steal and control our focus. The fortuity is that they allow us to multi-task, but is that really our goal? Sure, we can accomplish more things efficiently, but not without diminishing the quality of our performance. Our mindset would like us to believe that with multi-tasking we achieve more, but studies show the end results to be less valuable, less constructive, and less productive.

In as little as two seconds our memory can begin to fade. Shifting our concentration from one task to another for more than ten seconds can divert our attention for more than ten minutes before we regain the initial involvement we had with the first one. While racing in an attempt to try and achieve more, we are obviously focusing much less.

On more than one occasion I have witnessed people listening to music in the background, while on their cell phones, with paperwork spread out in front of them, as they're glancing up at a monitor, and even curiously trying to eavesdrop on another nearby conversation. It's inconceivable to me to presume we could possibly enjoy life to the fullest this way.

There is more to life than increasing its speed. —Gandhi

One of the most consequential distractions to our productivity can be television. A metaphor often used for this medium infers it can be bubblegum for the eyes. Even if we're extremely selective about what we watch, we can invest a disproportionate share of our time compared to the benefit we receive. A thirty-minute broadcast contains, at best, only twenty-two minutes of actual programming time, the balance consisting of commercials and advertisements. The ability to pre-record specific programs and advents like TiVo at least minimize the cost of sitting in front of the tube. Television can be extremely informative and educational; though, caution is the word as it can still act like a sieve for the few precious hours we have in a day.

We are a country recognized for its high levels of stress, anxiety disorders, and hypertension. Many physicians are in agreement that we need a stronger willingness to turn all our electronic buttons to their off position on occasion, possibly even removing them from our sight. There are moments when we need to be accessible, but certainly not twenty-four/seven. At some point, we are merely doing and not living, forgetting that we are human beings and not human doers.

As Americans, we sometimes return to work after a vacation with a sense of guilt, as though we may have left our co-workers down. On the contrary, many other countries actually require a minimum amount of vacation... not after the first year, but from day one. France, for example, mandates that all employees receive thirty-five days of vacation every year... from their "thirty-five-hour" workweek. Part of the decision lies in our preference between a higher standard of living and a higher quality of life.

Sometimes success entails more responsibility, and we feel the need to be more accessible. This is frequently only true to a point. Just because technology offers us access to more information and the ability to communicate so easily, doesn't necessarily imply that these are always valuable choices. At times we may give ourselves a false sense of importance, that we may be urgently needed. We get stuck on the same treadmill as many others around us. It's often been shown that when we don't respond to a problem immediately, by the time we do become involved it will already have resolved itself. We may even find that it was such a small predicament that it didn't really require our attention in the first place.

Below is what I sometimes demonstrate as the "Ninety Second Test." The goal is to see if you can complete everything required within the ninety-second time allotment. The only thing necessary to take this test is a pen, a blank sheet of paper, and a timepiece. And the only way you will really know if you can pass this test is to grab a pen and some paper now. It won't have the same impact if you merely read through it now with the hope of trying to take it at a later time.

Ninety Second Test

1. Read everything before you do anything.

2. Print your complete name at the top of your blank sheet of paper.

3. Circle your first name twice.

4. Draw six circles in the lower right hand corner of your page.

5. Put a different number in each of the circles.

6. Draw eight triangles in the lower left hand corner of your page.

7. Put a different letter in each of the triangles.

8. In the center of the page, multiply 987 by your age.

9. Now draw a double square around your answer.

10. Use your pen to punch five holes around your entire multiplication.

11. Now make three dots next to each hole you just made.

12. Draw two vertical lines down the right side of the page.

13. Draw three horizontal lines across the top of the page.

14. Make two stars after your last name.

15. Now that you have finished reading everything, as instructed in sentence number 1, do only sentence number 2.

Having completed the test, you should appreciate that there is a faster and easier way to finish on time upon better scrutiny to the instructions. Forcing ourselves to take time and focus, we can eliminate an oversight before we jump ahead too quickly. All too often we miss the essence of what we're actually trying to accomplish.

Think back to some of your most treasured memories before asking yourself... what enduring quality of life have I ever achieved at break neck speed? And secondly, what am I working for... what am I *really* working for?

Understanding these questions should make us ponder how much we might be missing ...as we multi-task and live our lives faster than we can pedal.

Your Attention Please

When we remove ourselves from cognitive awareness, our attention span tends to drift rather quickly. The average person can only sustain his or her focus for twenty to twenty-five seconds before unwillingly being distracted by something that appears to be of greater value.

Based on this understanding, any important thoughts we have are vulnerable until they're put in written form. They need protection from our wandering minds.

Let's say, for example, that in visiting a doctor's office you have three primary concerns about your health. Within moments of expressing your first concern, the doctor's thoughts may have already turned to qualifying questions and possible remedies, decreasing the amount of his or her listening that can be devoted to you simultaneously. As the doctor asks questions in return or renders possible solutions, you may also become distracted and veer away from your original three concerns. Having a few key words at your fingertips can help prevent your focus from straying haphazardly.

We can become a victim to our intrusive thoughts at any moment. We may be sitting in a meeting and though we're trying to be attentive, our minds continually escape to the golf course. Or, we're at the gym and find ourselves thinking more about food than the pounds we want to lose. A speaker asks us to consider the chart on his Powerpoint presentation. But our minds insist on reliving all the fun we had at the company party last night. Our minds love to wander. And especially when trying to be creative, we actually *want* them to wander. Again, keeping a couple key words in front of us will occasionally call our attention back to why we began brainstorming in the .

Because our perception thrives on making comparisons, it is unfair to expect our focus to remain targeted without intentional effort. Part of this could also be blamed on the fact that certain eye muscles can become fatigued, too.

Each eye is surrounded by six extra-ocular muscles that work together in pairs as they constantly search for new data. Aristotle first discovered an interesting example of eye muscle fatigue while watching a waterfall. After gazing at it and then looking away, the landscape appeared to move in the opposite direction than what the water had been flowing. The eyes had become fatigued in trying to watch the water, which then resulted in an artificial movement (in the opposite direction) of a stationary object.

A rotating spiral can duplicate this same illusion. When someone watches the spiral rotating inward for at least thirty seconds and then looks at another object, the second object now appear to visually grow up to five times its actual size. When this is repeated, this time rotating the spiral outward instead, the object will now appear to shrink almost five times smaller. This happens because once the eye muscles become fatigued in trying to keep up with the movement of the spiral, our brain loses its point of reference and the comparative size of another object becomes distorted.

As a young driver, I remember my brother once pulling up beside me at a stoplight. We each lowered our windows so that we could chat for a moment before the light changed. As we were looking at each other, my brother secretly put his car in reverse and slowly drifted backwards. My immediate reaction was to slam on my brakes since my impression was that I was drifting forward. He knowingly created a perfect illusion, based on Aristotle's discovery, which was worthy of a great laugh.

I was also reminded of "selective" visual fatigue during a trip to Africa, spent primarily in Tanzania. What a surreal environment... to witness hundreds of zebras running in the wild. In fact, the first time I saw one I was absolutely awestruck as I watched this magnificent animal in its natural habitat, trotting against a backdrop of open plains and acacia trees. For the first time in my life *I* was in the cage (our vehicle) and this beautiful creature was free to roam anywhere it desired.

As the week went on I saw countless herds of zebras. Each time I was overwhelmingly fascinated by the intricate color pattern they fashioned, no two alike. They were simply enchanting and seemed to project out of nature more than most other creatures we saw. But as the week went on it wasn't unusual to see thousands of them in one day, almost an endless number everywhere we looked. By the end of the week, when our guide would announce that we were approaching another crossing of them, I would barely look in their direction. I had become too jaded despite their natural beauty, as they were no longer a novelty. Even what we most desire to see can eventually become all too familiar.

Just like our vision, our hearing is perceptually selective, too. A man from the rural farmlands of Pennsylvania was visiting New York City and suddenly stopped in his tracks as he listened to the sound of a cricket hiding under a leaf. No one else near him could even hear it because they had never been "conditioned" to listen for it. But when several coins dropped out of someone's pocket, everyone on the street immediately turned to look toward the noise, as that was a more familiar sound.

What we seek out as having perceived value can often prevent us from living in the moment. Just like a mirage it constantly eludes us. If I only had a newer car, or if I just had a better paying job, or if I could only take three strokes off my game. . . as soon as we achieve any one of these, however often, it almost instantly becomes devalued and now all we seem to notice are all the boats larger than our own. Our satisfaction dissipates as soon as we've attained what we were after. And then our wants shift focus, again, as though what we already have is now invisible. By constantly looking too far ahead we can miss what is more relevant and valuable to us in the present.

No two people ever see precisely the same thing at any given moment. Because our bodies can never be exactly superimposed, each of us is viewing what we see from a slightly different perspective. More important, no two individuals ever perceive things the same way either, not even the same sentence. Our perception is as unique to us as our thumbprint. It is forever trying to interpret and categorize our world to assist us in making better sense of it. And because of that, our understanding of life consists of layers of patterns. To learn anything new and see things from a fresh perspective, we need to break those patterns.

The picture below shows a die with six spots on it. Or does it?

Our mind assumes that there are six spots because of the pattern that we are accustomed to seeing on dice and dominos. Even though we can't actually see a sixth spot, our perception automatically envisions where it should be beneath the hand. This is based on the patterns ingrained in us from seeing the same configuration before.

Since there are actually only *five* spots, we can also create the illusion of the four spot side of a die by instead placing our hand on the opposite side and covering up the middle spot. Now our mind innocently accepts that only four spots are present, never questioning that a fifth one is covered by our hand.

The same thing happens in the next sample. Our mind superimposes an additional spot under the hand and it looks like three.

Once, again, the empty space underneath the hand is overlooked. Our perception, based on our acceptance of patterns, assumes that another spot is present. In the same way, it would appear as one spot if we instead were to cover the opposite one in the corner.

We can intentionally lead someone along this same path as they create their own visual pattern. Try asking someone to spell the word coke. They will reply, "C-O-K-E." Now ask them to spell the word joke, and they will say, "J-O-K-E." Then ask them to spell poke, and they say "P-O-K-E." Finally, ask them to spell the white of an egg, and usually they'll reply, "Aha, you can't fool me, it's Y-O-L-K." However, the correct answer would really be "the white of an egg."

While each of us becomes locked into visual patterns, some are more rigid than others. The more proficient we become in breaking those patterns, the more potential we have for seeing what we're missing. Ancient civilizations had access to the same sand that we currently use to create silicon chips for storing information. However, the people of that time couldn't even begin to envision this outlandish possibility. There are undeniably more ideas for us to visualize and discover than we could ever imagine.

Do you live your life by rituals, or can you easily step away from a comfortable and methodical routine? What specific triggers are most beneficial in helping you to see something from a new vantage point? Even better than pondering about them is to "list" these triggers. They can act as a reminder and a catalyst when you need a nudge on occasion.

The Tone Zone

In our office I like to refer to the staff's over all personality as our attitude quotient. It's kind of a subjective scale as to how attentive, enjoyable, and memorable we can be in responding and servicing our patients' needs. My goal for our staff is that whenever someone calls our office, the caller is convinced that the person speaking with them is smiling.. just by the tone of their voice.

In the same way that a single car can stop a whole line of traffic, one lousy attitude in the office is enough to pull everyone else's down. At the pace of today's business, we only have a couple seconds to make a first impression. A person calling has no inference as to what is happening in our office either before or after the call. There is no inkling as to how chaotic it may be at times. I may only see some patients once in two years. During their scheduled time, we have a very narrow window to make their visit memorable. Each staff member has the ability to affect a patient's experience in a positive or negative way.

During part of my professional training, I had an enlightening experience working in an office that was the epitome of what *not* to do.

Primarily the fault of two people, their character alone was enough to trickle down and affect the mood of the entire office. Judging by their voices alone, it wasn't so much what was said, but in how it was said. The sincerity and compassion of someone's voice makes an enormous impression in how they are first perceived. It takes just one bad attitude among a room full of people to dramatically reduce the positive energy flow.

In a contrasting situation, while doing my residency in Los Angeles, I found myself in an office that was exactly the opposite. Every time a patient called, they were made to feel as though this was the most important conversation of the day. You could almost hear the smile through the phone and the patient felt sincerely welcomed before he or she ever arrived.

The entirety of any staff must be acutely aware of how every customer or patient sees the business or practice through their eyes. That way they can be made to feel as important as possible.

I remember changing banks some time ago just because of one teller. The bank was convenient, had competitive rates, and offered business accounts that met all of my needs. But having to continually deal with such a grumpy person day after day was depressing—the juice just wasn't worth the squeeze.

The movie titled *The Doctor*, starring William Hurt, is an excellent example of learning how to put yourself in someone else's place, especially in a healthcare setting. The more recent release of *The Ultimate Gift* also sets the stage for deciphering how to re-evaluate and adjust our attitudes toward more significant values, no matter what cards we are dealt.

How often do you *really* attempt to see things from another person's point of view? Are you easily affected by someone else's attitude?

Think about how your demeanor impacts on those you come in contact with. It is paramount to develop a confident way of compartmentalizing challenging situations so that you can always return to a positive state of mind.

QUESTION
WHAT YOU SEE

Distorted Reality

Quite often the focus of our decision making is based on something very different from what we believe we are seeking. When we go to the movies, we're not really there to watch Hollywood's latest technology for casting varieties of colored light on the screen of a dark room. We want to be entertained with an emotional storyline that makes us laugh or cry, and takes our imagination into a fantasy world.

We don't want a refrigerator as much as we want the convenience of a cold, refreshing drink whenever we're thirsty. We don't want glasses or contact lenses as much as we want clearer vision. What we really want is what something will *do* for us... not the item itself.

We like to assume that we make intelligent decisions based on actual facts. But we unknowingly justify many of our choices on more of an emotional level. We tend to accept common beliefs from the masses as truth and allow these "beliefs" to determine much of what we do. These eventually become our emotional reality as we gradually gain confidence in what we *think* they represent.

While we might consider something to be the best, in fact, it is only best in our own mind, a decision based on our own belief. If someone insists that the best ice cream they have ever had is Turkey Hill, then it definitely *is*... in the mind of that person. If a customer thinks it's a lousy vacuum cleaner, it *is* a lousy vacuum cleaner, at least to him or her. We presume that we are making wise decisions based on our education, our previous experiences, and our collective intelligence, even though they can be quite irrational.

A famous study was once conducted on Coke soft drink products more than a decade ago. Coke is one of the most widely recognized words in the world, among any language. This corporate giant already owned a dominating share of the market, and was hoping to expand itself even more. A new product was developed, with purportedly an even better formula, and they decided to name it New Coke. A blind study used to test its overall popularity found that the majority of customers liked the new taste even better.

Before long the supermarket shelves were jammed with the new-found product—but, unfortunately, that's exactly where it stayed. Nobody wanted to purchase it, even though it tasted "better." Coca-Cola had spent a small fortune developing, testing, marketing, and delivering the product to all its distributors, but no one wanted it. People were too committed to the original brand. They were emotionally attached to it and didn't want to sacrifice their confidence in something they already trusted and that satisfied their needs.

You can't judge a book by its cover... but people do.

The company marketing and advertising personnel were forced to quickly readjust their thinking, which led to the new campaign of what is now called Classic Coke. They learned the hard way that it doesn't matter what product is best. All that matters is what is best in the minds of the consumers. The public insisted on having the original formula. Even though the new formula tested better, again it wasn't what people wanted emotionally.

Not only do we make emotionally based decisions, but we also tend to believe we are very detail oriented. Especially when it comes to our vision, we see a lot less detail than we imagine. Our mind has the never ending chore of trying to formulate a picture from the many present and missing pieces in our view and then conceptualizing what we know as our perception. As referred to earlier, it is tirelessly making corrections and adjustments to compensate for the chaotic and fast moving world we live in.

As an example of just how efficient our visual perception is, look at the paragraph below. You will notice that all the letters appear jumbled together, making no sense at all. Surprisingly, though, you'll find you are able to read it without great difficulty, because your mind only ever sees part of an entire picture and is accustomed to creating a whole thought from very limited information.

Try your best to see how easily you can read the following paragraph.

Tihs mgiht seem almsot ipmosislbe to raed at frist.

But bceuase our mnid olny nedes to see prats

of wrods rtaher tahn ecah idnivdiaul lteetr,

you can raed it qutie esialy, eevn wehn

lokonig at tihs scarmbeld mses.

You might think that the person who wrote this was dyslexic. However, a prank from the University of Cambridge showed that a high percentage of viewers were able to read a paragraph similar to this one with little or no hesitation. All that was required was the first and last letters of every word be in the correct place. Again, because we are not as detail oriented as we believe, we are seeing merely an overview of what we scan. Our mind creates the majority of what we perceive. We believe we are seeing everything, but it's just an illusion.

We often become victims to our own environment in only seeing what we want to see. After we purchase a new car, suddenly we notice all the other models exactly like our own. Almost overnight they begin to show up everywhere, because we are inclined to look for what is already familiar to us.

An even better demonstration is to take a box of crayons and use a red crayon to write the word green and then use a blue crayon to write the word yellow. Continue this same process, using at least seven various colored crayons to write colors other than the color of the crayon you're holding. Now show the words to someone else and ask them to say the "colors" of the words out loud. They will have great difficulty "saying" the colors they see as their mind has developed a pre-disposition for "reading" them. Our perception takes over, again, and sees what's easiest to recognize, which is the word and not the color. We see in generalized pictures first. Only with conscious effort do we see in more detail.

I was reminded of an illusion in nature while in Africa when our guide told us to take notice of a particular sausage tree. It was approximately a hundred yards in front of us. The sausage tree is characterized by dangling pods at least three inches in diameter, giving the appearance of dozens of thick sausages hanging from its branches. I could barely see the individual pods in the distance except for the distinguishing shadows they created.

We were dumbfounded when our guide insisted that he could see a large creature relaxing in the tree. The tree appeared to be completely uninhabited, but we became very enthusiastic at the thought of seeing a leopard, one of the rarest animals to spot in the wild. This would certainly be the highlight of our week. Our guide was somehow able to discern its tail among the camouflage of all the other similar shadows from the hanging sausages. Out of eight passengers... none of us could see it.

Our vehicle came within twenty yards of the tree, still none of us could see even a silhouette of the leopard. Finally, after coming within a mere ten or twelve feet of the tree, we were now able to see this incredible animal leisurely watching the day pass from his perch.

His spots blended perfectly with the leaves and his tail with the sausage-like growths, creating the perfect camouflage for concealing him. The trained eyes of our guide knew exactly what to look for, while we could barely see it under his direction at close range.

Because our vision is pre-conditioned to only comprehending an environment already familiar to us, it takes an added effort to notice finer details from a new or unusual setting. Just a minimum of exposure allows us to adapt and accept the demands required for new visual conditioning. The only prerequisite is that we are willing to recognize there is something we fail to see and that we're open to looking from an unexplored perspective.

In the same way that our vision may be handicapped by what it hasn't been trained to see, our judgment can also be impaired by the generalizations we've come to accept. Our brain likes statistics and instinctively wants to categorize anything it possibly can, as it is easier to identify with our surroundings faster that way. For example, glaucoma is a disease generally found among the older population. Not long ago I examined a five-year-old patient who had gone blind in both eyes from glaucoma. Because of the rarity of glaucoma in someone so young, he had never been correctly diagnosed in time to save his vision. Much of his sight may have been saved had an earlier healthcare provider not assumed that his decreasing vision was probably something much less serious. The caveat is in knowing and recognizing that there is much to be seen beyond our traditional expectations.

Our perception is almost always self-limited with respect to our potential. Just for a moment, imagine what you would like to accomplish if there were no barriers in your way. Now, take a few more moments visualizing these aspirations without the roadblocks of time, knowledge, experience, and whatever else is standing in your way.

Our Mind's Eye

It is intriguing how much our perception governs our decision making process, especially when it allows us to become irrational. Imagine wanting to buy a certain movie. The price at a particular store is twenty dollars. A friend also advises you that just down the street, only three miles away, the same movie is on sale. It can be purchased at that store for only five dollars. Your immediate reaction may be that you'd be spending your money foolishly at this first location, paying four times the amount that you could be paying at the second. So, to save fifteen dollars, you drive a mere three miles and save the majority of the money you would have spent.

Now, let's say that a few weeks later you're in the same original store and this time you're considering buying a new large screen television. The price is two thousand dollars. Again, your trusting friend mentions that there's a sale up the street, only three miles away, and the sale price is only nineteen hundred and eighty-five dollars. Once more you can save fifteen dollars. This time, however, your gut instinct tells you not to bother wasting the time involved going to the other store because fifteen dollars would be a very small percentage of the two-thousand-dollar television already here. It doesn't seem worth the hassle of driving three miles.

In essence, each scenario offers you the capability of saving fifteen dollars, and in each case it requires driving the same distance to save the same amount of money. Our mind's eye seems to believe that it's a much better deal to save the money on the movie than the television, even though they require the exact same effort for the exact same amount of savings. Again, our value systems are often inconsistent because of the distorted ways that we use our perception to justify our decisions.

I heard about a woman who was visiting Spain, quite some time ago, while the famous artist Pablo Picasso was still alive. Coincidentally she found herself next to him in line at a checkout counter. When she suddenly realized who he was, she became inundated with excitement. "Oh my gosh, you're Mr. Picasso. I can't believe that you're standing right here in person. Oh, I would give anything for a piece of your artwork. Please, could you draw a little something for me? Anything at all?" she inquired.

"Ma'am," he replied, "I have nothing with me to draw and this is probably not the most ideal environment for me to try and create something artistic."

"But, please," she insisted, "anything you can possibly imagine would be wonderful." She reached into her purse and pulled out a crumpled napkin along with a hotel pen. She offered them to him saying, "Here, please just sketch whatever pops into your mind. Just to have a scribble of anything that strikes you will be fine."

So he looked out the window and drew his impression of a scene across the street. After little more than thirty seconds he handed the napkin back to her as he said, "How is that? Are you satisfied now?"

"Yes, oh my gosh, that's wonderful," she blurted. "How much do I owe you?"

After a moment of thought he replied, "That will be 100,000 pesetas (approximately 1,500 U.S. dollars)."

The woman looked up in shocked disbelief. "What?" she stammered. "100,000 pesetas? That's an enormous sum of money for just a few seconds of your time."

Picasso now peered into her eyes intently, and with a slight smirk at the corner of his mouth he answered, "Yes, but it took me an entire life time to learn how to do that."

I later learned Picasso began bartering more often from that very experience. Sometimes, after dining in the most expensive restaurants of the city, he would offer a simplistic sketch with his signature to the restaurant owner as a proposition to pay for his meal. Depending upon our point of reference, our perspectives can be easily influenced by our own perceived values.

Likewise, our perception of marketing can be misconstrued, too, as we confuse features for benefits. The manufacturer may advocate that their Longshot Golf Ball is made from a new core design, but this is only a feature. The company may even tout that you'll be able to hit it forty yards farther, which is a nice advantage, but only an advantage.

What you really want to know is its benefit for you, and the benefit is that it will lower your score.

After a long round of golf, our emotions may tell us that we "need" a beer. But, sadly to admit, a beer is merely a *feature* of the clubhouse. If you played in extreme heat and are completely dehydrated, the true *benefit* of the clubhouse is that it also has the necessary water needed for re-hydration. Another advantage is that, after drinking all that beer, it also has a restroom.

While it may sound counterproductive, there are actually occasions when we want to intentionally distort our perception. We often use purposeful distractions to make a particular situation seem less lengthy or painful. Imagine a young child sitting in a doctor's office about to receive an injection. Many times a doctor or nurse will use stuffed animals, an interesting story, or even a free gift to remove a child's focus from the ensuing pain of a needle. When we need incentive for going to the gym, we often rely on music or television to make a long and monotonous workout more palatable.

Employers may induce their staff to focus on specific goals through bonuses, competitions, and incentive rewards. Or often we're invited to business events and meetings where free food, giveaways, and a celebrity speaker are the motivation for our attendance. Innovative businesses will use a wide variety of attention-getting themes in exchange for the time to share their message or propaganda with an appropriate audience.

I remember a firsthand experience when I intentionally wanted to distort my own perception. During my graduate work, I had to work with human cadavers to better understand the relationships between our eyes and systemic diseases. As an introduction to the class, we started with baboons since they are similar in anatomical structure to that of humans. Afterward, we began our study with the human cadavers upside down, not having to stare at an actual face right from the start. Eventually, we continued our work with them face up, though not before assigning them silly names. This was not meant in disrespect, but to make light of and lessen the impact that the object we were working with was once a true, living person. Changing our perception helped us to remove ourselves emotionally so that we could focus on our priority of learning.

If you've ever listened to music or a book while driving, you are already familiar with the value of distraction, to make your travel time seem shorter. What other ways can you alter your focus *intentionally* to create more leverage in achieving your goals?

Just Like Magic

As an illusionist, I have a deep appreciation for how easily our perceptions can become distorted. Ironically, we assume that what happens in the hands of a skilled entertainer is responsible for deceiving our natural logic when in fact, most of what appears to be happening is artificially created in the minds of the audience. The performer is simply taking advantage of the peculiarities in the way we typically process information.

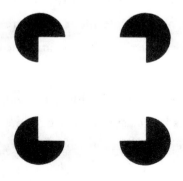

Notice in the picture to the left how our mind artificially creates a square that seems to float above the incomplete circles. Because our vision has been conditioned to recognize common shapes as opposed to irregular ones, we much prefer to imagine these as complete circles with another object obscuring our view rather than as four asymmetrical spots.

Place your hand over one or two of these shapes. The illusion disappears, and you instantly see them for what they really are.

This same illusion becomes even more pronounced when we add an extra element of color. Can you appreciate that the invisible square is now even more evident?

Magic as entertainment is an ideal metaphor for the study of human behavior and the way our perception responds to what we "think" we see. There is an endless array of false perceptions that we instinctively create on our own, based on our known reality. True, an illusionist may tip the scales in his or her favor with well-rehearsed timing and technique. However, much of our bewilderment has more to do with misguided observations, our perceived awareness, and the general assumptions we make.

For instance, when a performer places an object in his hand and closes his fingers around it, our mind bases its decision as to where the object is on the naturalness of the movement. We look at what appears to have happened visually and whether or not it logically makes sense.

This gives the opportunity for numerous methods to be explored for disrupting the logical conclusions of what the spectators see.

While certain actions may be cleverly disguised and go completely unnoticed, others may be presented very blatantly and deliberately as alternative means are incorporated to challenge the senses. Ultimately, what appears to be happening and what actually takes place are usually two distinctly different entities.

There is a common term among magicians known as "misdirection." Essentially, it means misguiding someone's focus. I believe a more suitable term would be "visual direction," especially because an audience will typically look wherever the magician looks. When a performer has mastered the ability to have people look exactly where he or she wants them to, preferably away from a secret action that may be taking place, he or she is causing them to focus in a specific direction of choice.

A seasoned performer is also an actor who can direct the attention of the audience to precisely where the lines between illusion and reality become blurred. The laws of science, physics, and especially psychology all play a credible role as they lend themselves to enhancing our false perception. Just like the earlier examples with the spots, our vision is quick to accept the obvious and makes many assumptions because we can't see everything at once. An illusionist can play on those assumptions and purposely help to construct our reality incorrectly.

Here's a fundamental example of how our perception overrules the way we interpret what we see.

Use three of your own business cards. On the back of one of them write: Please Take This One With You. Now turn it over again so that all three cards are front side up. Keep the one with the message on the reverse side in the middle.

To perform this "magical" prediction, spread the three cards out in front of someone and ask them to push one of the cards toward you. (Lay them out very casually, with the printed sides up, knowing that the middle one is the one with the message on the back.) If they push the middle one toward you, take the other two away and turn them over, blank side up. Then say to the person, "That is the one you chose, and the one I'd like you to keep. In fact, it even says so on the reverse side," as you turn it over for them to see your prediction.

If they push one of the end ones toward you, say, "Fine. Now with your other hand, I'd like you to pick up one of two remaining cards." If they pick up the center one, pull the other one toward you, too, and say, "The only one remaining in your hand is the one I'd like you to keep; it even says so." Again, turn it over for them to see your prediction as you show the others to be blank.

If, however, they pick up the other end one, say, "Please hand that one to me, too. Now there's only one you haven't touched, the only one left for yourself. That is the one I'd like you to keep anyway. It even says so on the back." Turn it over to reveal that it's the only one with your predicted message.

Obviously you can only do this once, because you are using different sequences to arrive at the same conclusion. The key is that the spectator doesn't realize this because he or she has no frame of reference. In demonstrating this, it will be quite convincing you were able to predict the outcome, or you had complete control over the card they would select. Even though the secret is elementary (as many illusions are) the impression you create in the mind of a spectator can be quite bewildering. This not only provides an intriguing way to offer someone your business card, but it increases the likelihood that he or she will keep it.

Because we think in patterns, there are many instances when it's easier to fool an adult than a child. Children haven't developed many of these structured paradigms yet, which allows them to observe things in a less biased way than someone with years of imbedded experience. Because we subconsciously depend upon our previous life experiences to make new and better decisions, we have a tendency to block our own free thinking. And this, in turn, lends itself nicely to the art of deception.

A classic example of this is demonstrated within the following pictures using the same card you saw earlier. It's actually possible to represent different numbers just by holding the same card in various positions. The first picture represents a three, and the second one represents a four. Can you decipher how each one of these numbers is determined?

Here are two more examples. The first one represents a two, and the last one represents a one.

Now do you see which aspect of the picture is most critical for creating a number? If you still can't detect it, try disregarding the entire card itself and observing the only thing left in the picture that can possibly make the distinction. Sometimes we become so overly focused that we miss the fundamental and obvious answer.

Occasionally if we look at something too intently, we can actually make it more problematic to comprehend than it should be. It may not surprise you then that many preschoolers are faster at discovering the pattern for creating the numbers above than the average adult. Our instinct is to look at something about the picture itself, or possibly its orientation. The number of fingers holding the card, irrespective of which way it's held, is what accounts for the numerical value.

An illusionist is only successful when we accept a misguided conclusion based on our perception that something appears to be true. The surprising irony is that each and every day our entire understanding of the world around us is constructed in the same way. Because our perception creates our reality, it is quite different for each of us. Reality is just an illusion in and of itself.

In very much the same way, we can be ever so close to achieving one of our goals and yet not see the opportunity hovering right in front of us. We may be staring directly at a unique and empowering idea, yet somehow it is still invisible. Just because our perception is so easily distorted, we don't want to miss or neglect the obvious.

Each of us is guilty of unknowingly fabricating a continual array of our own illusions on a daily basis. Our fictional reality is highly subliminal, and this confusion becomes more deeply entrenched with age. It is nothing more that our perception playing on what it believes it already knows.

The best way to get your arms around this thought process is to test the above "finger experiment" on several friends. Just make sure you word your instructions to them correctly and you use a sizeable picture, so that your finger changes are not too conspicuous. In the same way we often learn more by instructing others, you'll appreciate a better understanding of this concept by being on the demonstration end.

In Disguise

If our perception is such a predominant factor in how we see our world, is it ever possible to understand a true picture of ourselves? Is there any way to know how we appear to others? Interestingly, who we are is what we think other people think we are. In other words, our own impression of ourselves is based upon what we feel other people think of us. This may be entirely different than what they *really* think.

If you've ever listened to a recording of your own voice, you'll have to admit that it sounds much different than the way you are accustomed to hearing yourself speak. Or, if you ever had a caricature drawn of yourself, or a candid photo taken at an unusual moment, the experience may be equally unexpected. Another person will see particular features of your character or physical appearance as more magnified or minimized than you do. If so much of what we see around us is distorted, then even more of how we perceive ourselves is distorted. Again, we think we are what we think other people think we are.

I am as guilty as the next person of making assumptions about someone else too hastily on occasion. Most studies agree that we are apt to make an inherent judgment within the first ten seconds of seeing someone for the first time. It could stem from something about the person's character, affability, or overall attitude. But in many cases, it can be unfairly based on our misconceptions or preconceived notions.

I clearly remember my first impression upon meeting a particular celebrity football player. While not in the NFL, this respected athlete played in a semi-professional league. These teams travel throughout the country playing full tackle football in complete uniforms, pads, and helmets in front of an enthusiastic fan base. The part that was almost unconceivable to me was that beyond being of rather small stature, she was a *great-grandmother*. Not just content to race her five great-grandchildren across their yard, Charlotte Chambers played as a safety every weekend for the Orlando Starz.

Born premature and into a poverty stricken family, Charlotte was never expected to survive. The neighbors would stop by every morning curious to know whether the ill-fated infant was still alive. She beat all the odds against her and became extremely physically able. As a youth she participated in various sports, primarily softball and track.

Down the road, at the tender age of sixty-eight, this petite little lady again resorted to sports to help take her mind away from the loss of her mother.

When meeting her off the gridiron, most onlookers fall into the same category I did in wanting to completely misjudge her capabilities due to the small size of her frame and her age. I had the delightful pleasure of being proven wrong as I caught up with her while she was working out and pumping iron at her local gym. She forcibly insists, "It's never too late to start something you enjoy." At a time when many of her peers were reaching for their canes, she preferred to reach for a football and take on an improbable challenge where she became one of the heroes of her team.

One of the greatest pleasures in life is doing what people say you cannot.

Another case in point that stands out even more to me, as a sports enthusiast, happened while I was volunteering a small amount of my time at a summer camp program for burn victims. I met a charming young girl that looked at life as though she were witnessing a rainbow every minute. She had a persona that could make anyone smile regardless of how many adversities you could lay on her plate.

In merely exchanging conversation, you would never gather that much of her life had been restricted to her wheelchair. Intentionally disfigured from domestic violence, Gabby had no arms or legs because more than eighty percent of her body had been severely burned. It almost seemed even more unjust that she was there to participate in an active sports-oriented camp specifically for young burn victims. As difficult as it might have been for the other burn victims to actively play, I imagined that it had to be especially taxing and disappointing for Gabby. My thoughts were limited to: how could she conceivably participate during the scheduled soccer game that afternoon?

Once, again, I was completely blindsided as Gabby proved herself to be more remarkable and inspiring on the soccer field than I could have ever predicted. It would be nearly impossible to describe what I saw, her wheelchair empty on the sidelines. She was astonishingly and intriguingly able to roll her body and maneuver the ball forward, unlike anyone I had ever seen, whenever it came close to her.

As the saying goes, you can't tell the size of the fight by the size of the person. As much as we endeavor not to, we constantly and mistakenly prejudge our own potential as well as others. And, unfortunately, it happens more often than we realize.

A simple and yet revealing exercise about yourself is to ask an acquaintance, someone who does not know you very well, to write down five or six character traits about you that seem immediately apparent to him or her. You also agree to do the same for the other person before exchanging the lists. Next, spend a few moments in conversation discovering something about the other individual that you would never have guessed. You will not only be surprised about your preconceived notions, but will likely learn something from a blind perspective that may even introduce you to a new side of yourself.

In the same way our perception can be self-limiting to our own achievements, it can be equally self-limiting to others. One of the greatest gifts we have to offer is in not being presumptuous about ours or anyone else's true potential.

SECTION 2:
PROGRESSIVE THINKING (DIRECTION)

IT'S NOT WHAT YOU SEE—

IT'S WHAT YOU *DON'T* SEE.

CHAPTER FOUR

SEE WHAT YOU'RE MISSING

When Wrong Is Right

Much of our education is competitive and revolves around knowing as many right answers as possible. Often our trusted manmade laws for the likes of science, physics, and economics prove themselves to be too self-limiting.

It's easy to convince ourselves that we have already reached the limit when we feel that something cannot be accomplished any faster, made to smaller tolerances, or produced more economically. But, over time, we continue to disprove what was once set in stone. The world is full of infinite possibility, even though society tries to frequently remind us that we should be accepting of what we already know.

Rules are made for people who aren't willing to make up their own.

At its first conception, a new idea may appear to be totally absurd. Then eventually, with enough ventured thinking, we begin to consider it as a true possibility. By the time it has reached fruition, we have already accepted it as common knowledge.

Imagine someone walking into a boardroom twenty years ago and saying, "I have a great marketing idea. Let's give all the latest models of our cell phone inventory away for free." There's a good chance the person would have been fired in a New York minute. In fact, I have a friend and fellow physician who owned one of the first true "pocket phones" in my area. He paid $3200 for it and was delighted beyond belief... at the time. That phone is now a member of the dinosaur era as even the newest ones are almost outdated before they hit the market.

More recently companies have been glad to offer their phones for free in exchange for a contract for their service. From software to pharmaceutical products to food samples, businesses were willing to give away free products in hopes of luring someone's interest and repeat business.

The twenty-first century has brought us an enormous amount of digital information at very marginal costs, and available at our fingertips. The constant focus and challenge now is to gain the consumer's attention and give information away for free, knowing that they may be interested in a higher caliber of information at a cost. At one time, it was all about making a sale. Today's most valued resource is a person's contact information, such as an email address, for repetitive marketing and the potential for multiple sales.

Mainstream thinking has been turned on its head. Not too long ago it was considered totally unprofessional and unethical for a physician or an attorney to advertise. Today, if you peruse the Yellow Pages (before they become extinct) for any given city, you'll likely find more ads for attorneys, doctors, and hospitals than you will for restaurants. In fact, you'll probably find ongoing sections of full-page ads that overshadow every other subtitle.

I typically see more billboards advertising hospital services and facilities than I do for any other business category in most communities. Until recently this, too, was considered an unethical way to promote healthcare. Now it's not only commonplace, but also essential for survival. Our own artificial constraints of logic made this unthinkable for quite some time. Then, almost overnight, the thought of breaking traditional thinking became acceptable.

Please understand that I am not condoning or condemning any specific form of self-promotion. I am merely pointing out this significant modification of our accepted logic and preconceived notions. Our inherent inventiveness is often overshadowed by the traditional and invisible codes of society.

Take a moment to study the maze in the next diagram. Which is the fastest direction you can take to make your way from point A to point B?

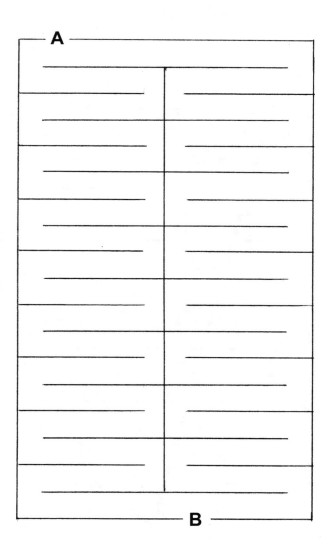

It ought to be fairly obvious that one direction will take you there more quickly, but which one is it? If you think you have identified which path is most direct, see if it coincides with the one drawn on the next page.

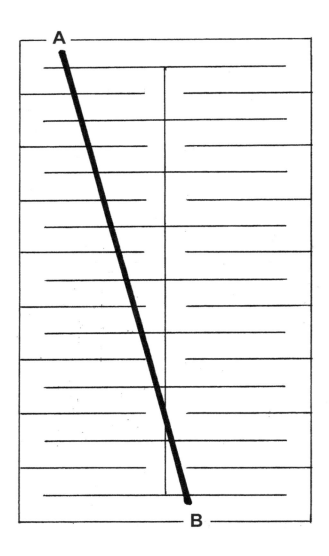

By drawing a straight line from point A to point B, you have still completed the task correctly. Perhaps, like the majority of people, you assumed that you had to stay inside the lines and weren't permitted to cross any of them. But this was never mentioned as a restriction. Our instinctive methodology for problem solving typically guides us to a more traditional and expected way of doing things.

If we were restricted from touching the lines, there is still an alternate path that satisfies our goal. It's still much faster to go around the maze, from A to B, without having to negotiate all the pathways within it.

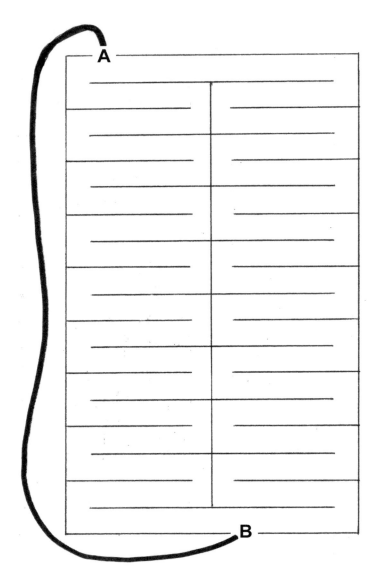

Again, we might be too quick to visualize that a path means traveling through the maze as opposed to simply going around it.

Would you be amazed if I told you that there was an even faster way to get from point A to B? Okay, how could there possibly be a faster way than the two alternatives already explained? (Take a moment to think about a plausible answer before reading ahead.) Well, if you tore the page out of the book and folded it so that point A was right next to the B, almost touching, it would now take a fraction of the time to draw a much shorter line. Again, our minds can become road blocked from previous exposures we've already had to similar challenges.

The person most responsible for limiting our choices and giving in to caution is the one you always see in the mirror. It all comes down to our willingness to break the mold.

Only dead fish swim with the current.

There was a time when football consisted of strictly a running and kicking game. Once teams began experimenting with the concept of the forward pass (which wasn't restricted but just never fully explored), they realized that they could move the ball much farther and with less brutal effort. Some early teams were able to exploit this to their demoralizing advantage. The skills to defend against a choice of receivers had not yet been developed. This is comparable to the development of the butterfly stroke in swimming, which was born out of not conforming to the traditional breaststroke... another way of challenging conventional wisdom.

Who would have ever considered that today's technology would be searching for new energy sources within raindrops, bridge vibrations, or the beating of our own hearts? Again, until we confront our time-trusted way of thinking, we will never truly appreciate what might be possible through innovative experimentation. An ideal practice is to sporadically give ourselves a license to dream and search for alternative ways to see what others simply take for granted.

Reason to Celebrate

Without a doubt, the biggest common denominator among the most successful people I've ever met is their willingness to make mistakes. In fact, while speaking with many of these influential people personally, they insisted that if they had to live their lives over again, not only would they make more mistakes, they would make them sooner, too.

Very few people in business go straight to the top. There are peaks and valleys and learning curves in practically everything we do. Both in business and pleasure, our lives are essentially a continuous journey of educational opportunities. The sooner we realize and admit that we are bound to make mistakes along the way, the faster we will accept them as learning experiences, adapt to our new found information, and prosper from the experience.

One of the optimal paths we can take is to actually "encourage" ourselves to make mistakes, which only means we will be learning faster rather than just stifling ourselves about what to do next. We should celebrate failure as a new pivotal point for aiming ourselves in a new and better direction. Even when we feel defeated, we never really lose as long as we remember the lesson.

> **Success is a lousy teacher; it seduces people into thinking they can't lose.**
> —Bill Gates

Step back for a moment to look at the scoreboard of success. In reality it's all a percentage game. If we only have one idea, there's a very slim chance that it will ever reach its full potential. However, if we have a hundred ideas, our chances for success increase dramatically.

The concept of failure is solely based on our own interpretation of a given outcome. The neurochemistry we possess supplies us with what we need to survive and thrive. Our brains were cleverly designed with enough dopamine, norepinephrine, and serotonin to rebound after failing, since it's a natural part of our growth process... as a child or as an adult. Think of these as nature's provision, a reserve for helping us to cope and thrive, despite the never-ending challenges we face.

In the process of learning new information, the microanatomy of the brain resembles miniature fireworks exploding in all directions as millions of connecting pathways share electronic impulses. Amazingly, these very same explosions also occur during our mistakes and failures, which implies that we are learning on a very similar scale, even when we're wrong.

Not long ago, I met a fascinating person who shared a first-hand story about several of his classmates from his early school years. His friends spent the vast majority of their spare time playing music rather than engaging in their schoolwork. Eventually, they summoned the courage to audition for a professional recording, but were turned down by Decca Records. Their same audition tape was subsequently turned down again and again, by Pey, Phillips, Columbia, and HMV. After prolonged discouragement from knocking on countless doors, a company named Parlophone finally decided to "give them a shot." The boys' persistence finally paid off, as they became known as the most influential band in rock and roll history... the Beatles.

As the gentleman continued sharing stories while we sat in The Cavern, the very club where the Beatle's legacy began, I was intrigued by the mystique of the ever so simple surroundings. It was just another reminder that great accomplishments are made by ordinary people with extraordinary passion and stamina.

We're inclined to believe that most successful people either stem from a sound education, a well-connected family, or an uncanny stroke of luck. While this has been readily disproved, what they do share in common is an incessant nature to challenge what we normally take for granted. They are willing to attack life knowing they may fail many times before satisfying their curiosity. We never know when just one more attempt will be the one that makes a difference.

Success doesn't come from perfection, but it does come from perseverance. I'm reminded of this every time I stumble upon an advertisement for Dyson vacuum cleaners. Their distinguishing features are that they are completely bag-less, more maneuverable (resting on a rotating ball rather than wheels), and filter household air. But even with these advantages, James Dyson couldn't convince any manufacturer to take his invention seriously.

After more than fifteen years of knocking on corporate doors, he finally gave up on the corporate giants and decided to sell it himself. Today his product dominates both the U.S. and European markets. With sales approaching a billion dollars a year, he can easily afford his lifestyle of a thirty-five million dollar mansion. Not bad for someone who was trained as an artist and, therefore, made his first prototype out of cardboard and duct tape. Even so, it took more than five thousand attempts to refine his idea before it became an undeniable success.

If you've ever caught a single snowflake on your hand, you know that its weight is imperceptible. The frozen particle is so light that the least hint of your breath is enough to send it flying or melt it away. During a snowfall millions upon millions of snowflakes may find a spot on the branch of a tree as they seemingly cling to each other. If it snows long and hard enough, eventually one *single* flake will make the difference in the branch succumbing to the weight as it falls to the ground.

There are numerous stories of people on an apparently endless journey in hopes of reaching their goals, never knowing if the fifty-seventh or three hundredth attempt will offer the solution they're seeking.

The "guaranteed" way to success is to always try one more time.

Several years ago I was invited to lecture in Japan for a very diverse group of business entrepreneurs. While they were very appreciative of the concepts and ideas I shared with them, I was equally enthralled to learn about one of their cultural traditions that they shared with me.

They explained that when their students enter our equivalent of first grade, each one is given a handful of bamboo seeds. They are instructed to go outside and plant their seeds near the classroom window where they can watch them grow. Each day they are encouraged to water and nourish them as they learn the value of enduring care for their infant plants. The children typically take this responsibility very seriously as they look forward to witnessing one of nature's miracles in the maturation of a simple seedling.

I thought back to my own experience as a first-grade student, remembering my own little Styrofoam cup with a lima bean seed. Within weeks I could see the fragile shoots spring up and the spider like roots descending. It was somewhat enchanting to watch this day by day as a youngster.

Unfortunately, these children in Japan don't have the luxury of sharing in the same excitement. They water and fertilize their plants, day after day, but nothing happens. They get to the end of the entire school year, yet still, nothing happens. As they leave for the interim break between grade changes, they are instructed to return each day and continue to nurture each other's plants. And when they arrive at the beginning of second grade, still the naked earth stares back at them.

I remember how lacking my own patience was at that age, so I assume that these children all feel like failures. Their instructor, however, insists that they keep tending to the plants and taking precious care of them. They continue to do so all through second grade, as well as all through third grade. I'm sure by this point they feel dejected, as though all their efforts have been worthless. My mind, at least, would have been distracted to all of the more entertaining aspects of child-hood. Obsessing over non-growing plants would have seemed futile, but these children are reminded to look after them every day.

They continue to do so all through fourth and fifth grades, yet not one bud ever merges from the unbroken soil. The ground where they planted their seeds looks the same as it always has, for what now is already half of their young life.

Finally, at the beginning of sixth grade, after more than five years of attending their seeds, these bamboo plants suddenly and miraculously grow over ninety feet in just six short weeks. Imagine the lesson these children would lose if they weren't encouraged to be adamant about their little botany project. For a young student, this becomes a powerful and life changing lesson for understanding patience as well as persistence.

> **A person who is a
> master of patience
> is a master of
> everything else.**

I keep a laminated advertisement of a game called "Wordthief" on my desk so that it's plainly visible. The game entails creating your own words and stealing other player's words with the use of individual cards that display a single letter. Not only is it fun and a great way to increase your vocabulary, but it won the National Parenting Center Seal of Approval, the Toy Testing Council Three Stars Award, the British International Toy Fair Best New Game, and was recognized as one of the Best 100 Games by Games Magazine.

So why do I always keep it in plain sight? It's because my friend Marty and I invented the game over twenty years ago and didn't pursue the prospect of marketing it with enough endurance. We looked into patent laws and the channels required for promoting it on a national level. But, while still busy in college, we reluctantly decided not to commit to the necessary time it would involve.

In the meantime, we had taught many other friends at Penn State how to play it under our own chosen name of "Squabble" (since we often used Scrabble pieces to play). So, either someone from college took more initiative to promote it than we did, or more likely someone else coincidentally came up with the exact same idea on their own. Either way, it became a lost opportunity because we weren't persistent in seeking its potential. My laminated advertisement reminds me to at least retain the lesson.

What simplistic and personal reminder could be meaningful to you for encouraging your own focus to stay on track in times of adversity?

Distorted View

All too often we permit ourselves to become overwhelmed and allow stress to manifest our lives. Then before we know it, the F word begins sneaking into our vocabulary. Unfortunately this F word, also known as "fear," is easily misunderstood. Essentially, fear is nothing more than a byproduct of change. Something new or different is happening, and we are not yet sure how to respond to it. It can become an exaggerated and unqualified part of our decision-making in what, or what "not," to do.

The famous illusionist Harry Houdini contended that our imagination not only magnifies our fear, but it is actually the primary cause of it. If we can just condition ourselves to reduce our levels of fear, we can accomplish many new forms of success. It would almost seem like magic to someone trapped in his or her own mindset.

Fear is most often a distorted perspective perceived as truth.

We commonly buy more than what we really need because we're afraid we might not have enough. Or, we miss out on a memorable experience because we're afraid we don't have enough time or the knowledge to try something new. Fear is simply the emotions we experience when we don't know the specific outcome. It's a part of our vocabulary that can be very deceiving, since it is usually nothing more than a distortion of our reality. It can ruin our confidence and rob us from our ability to flourish. If we think back to all the fears of our past, we find that the vast majority of them never came close to materializing.

If it seems that we are forever dwelling over the fears of the unknown, it's partially because fear is also a multi-billion dollar business in society. Vitamins to better vehicle tires to pet insurance, we are constantly reminded of what we should be doing to protect ourselves. What if this happened or that ever occurred? We sometimes obsess over the latest trends in clothing, the newest electronic gadgets, and the most popular way of dieting, for fear that society won't accept us as we are. Much of what we look upon as advertising is also an opportunity to prey on our fears.

Unfortunately, a sizeable amount of what we purchase is more out of fear than pleasure. We will probably need this some day, or we should take advantage of the special price since it's now on sale. Soon after our purchase, we shift into a defensive mode since we need to justify our hasty decision. We don't want to admit we were irrational or succumb to buyer's remorse.

On the other side of the coin we may be afraid to make a purchase. Would you purchase a toy for your eight-year-old if the labeling advised that it could be harmful to your child, with a risk of eye injuries and even death if not used properly? Not to mention that it's prone to injuring bystanders and can damage surrounding areas when used indoors. If you're a responsible parent you will have to make an executive decision on this one, because the label came attached to a jump rope.

The Wright brothers began their business as bicycle repairmen. When they developed their interest in flying, they also prepared for a long stage of trial and error. Knowing there would be an extensive learning curve, they purposely chose Kitty Hawk for all their flight attempts, since the sand there would be more forgiving. While not afraid, they were intuitive enough to anticipate a lengthy period of failures and equally excited to learn something new and valuable from each experiment. This is what gave them the momentum to continuously trudge forward. Obviously their thinking paid off, as ultimately they were successful. This is not the likely success story one might expect from a boy (Orville) who was expelled from sixth grade. His behavior may have been inappropriate at times but he wasn't afraid to fail.

Something as simple as taking a wrong turn while you're driving is a learning opportunity for knowing how to shorten your trip *next* time. If the fastest learners are the ones willing to make *more* mistakes *quicker*, how many ideas do you have on the back burner that you could at least attempt instead of procrastinating?

Hidden Value

At first thought, you may feel that winning the lottery would be the simplest way to solve all your problems. Ironically, however, it would undoubtedly impose a whole new set of challenges. Sure, you wouldn't mind that hassle; it's nice not having any concerns about whether or not you can afford something. However, there is a hidden price to pay for this uncommon luxury. It may appear to be the fastest way to easy street, but it doesn't come without its headaches.

It's difficult to put a dollar value on our education and experiences, and even tougher to put one on our attitude and emotions... the determining factors that make us happy. Winning the lottery might offer someone a more expensive lifestyle and a sense of freedom, but our perception can be very shortsighted in confusing quantity for quality.

Think of the many celebrities and noteworthy people you've read about who fell into an enormous amount of money, only to become distracted from the real values of living. That kind of lifestyle change is only healthy if you know how to keep your core values in perspective. If you are a poor money manager or decision maker now, more money can definitely complicate things even further. The lottery is a fairly poor investment to begin with... the odds essentially make it a tax on people who aren't very good at math.

Not long ago, one of my former high school teachers won $20.3 million in the Lottery. While it did provide him with enormous security, it also helped to extinguish the love of his career as a teacher and, at least initially, tarnished his ability to reach out to students the way he traditionally had in the past. Not the instigator of his change in fate (he had not even purchased the winning ticket himself), the responsibilities and inherent changes that suddenly arose were unforeseen. In many ways, his life had been equally rewarding and notably more manageable before he had won.

A good friend of mine began his career in retail sales. Then one day he decided to zero in on his instinctive talent as a salesperson. Rather than remain in an arena of lower cost products, he channeled all his efforts into a very specialized industry involving multi-million dollar equipment. A knack for inimitable customer relationships and a willingness to dream big opened the door for not only purchasing the company itself, but growing it ten fold from where it began. Today his business is well respected and a major supplier within the concrete building industry. Yet, his understated lifestyle and exemplary fairness to all his associates demonstrate his balanced priorities, which ulti-mately define his happiness and contentment. His practices of quality decision-making and the sharing of his success spill into his avocations, personal friendships, and generosity in giving back to society.

The way to make better decisions is to make more of them.

Still another most fascinating friend defines success as the freedom to work on his own time clock, while incorporating the opportunity to travel worldwide. By strategically combining his expertise in graphic design with an isolated niche market within the entertainment industry, he's been able to explore untold exotic places that are off most people's radar. The decision to let his passion drive his motivation means he never has to face his dread of going to a nine-to-five job.

The average person seldom gives much credible thought to devis-ing their ideal scenario for a livelihood. Studies show that six months after winning the lottery the difference in the increased level of hap-piness of the winner is less than we would guess. There's no doubt that financial freedom can offer more independence and affordability. But rather than reduce our anxieties... they simply change. If we had an annoying personality before, we will probably still have one after winning. Simply having more money doesn't guarantee that we will find more meaning and purpose in what we do. We gain our true colors and depth of character, our curiosity for the mysteries that life has to offer, by unleashing our hidden capabilities.

Probably the most outrageous comparison I can recall is an individual who has always been a fanatic about riding roller coasters. While it seemed almost ludicrous at the time, he decided to fashion an entire career out of riding these exhilarating forms of entertainment. For quite some time his small company would release a new book every year describing and comparing the best and the worst of these rides at various amusement parks across the country. He compared their height, speed, smoothness, fear factor, length of wait, cost, etc., to help other coaster enthusiasts make better decisions about where they might like to venture on vacation. He's another great example of adapting his work to his passion, even while earning a modest living.

Better perception always leads to better decision-making. It's easy to believe that we make our decisions based on reality. But our perceptual flaws interfere more often than we realize. If we make poor decisions without money, we will also most likely make poor decisions with it. Winning the lottery over night doesn't make us better decision makers. My former teacher commented that while it was temporarily exciting to win such a huge sum of money, it altered his life more than it improved his life. More valuable than winning any lottery were his family, friends, and health, as well as his education, memorable experiences, and having a sense of purpose.

Sure, we've read that money doesn't buy happiness, and we're taught that money isn't everything. But the significant lessons of life seldom arise out of a book or the classroom. It may help to "hear" an elaborate explanation, or to "see" an ultimate example. Although to fully comprehend something we must "experience" a real life situation for ourselves. You can listen to someone tell you how to swim or watch a detailed instructional video, yet never comprehend how it really feels to move as we stay afloat. Each of us learns in different ways and in various chronological orders. Many challenges that we face don't offer the opportunity of education before we need it; so we are forced to learn through trial and error.

Experience is a hard teacher – giving the test first, and the lesson last.

As young students my friends and I participated in a wide variety of sports. Among us there was one kid desperate to play basketball for the school team, despite never quite having the height and ball handling mechanics necessary to compete at that level of play. He tried out in seventh, eighth, and ninth grades, but was always cut from the roster. Once in high school, he put more effort than ever into practicing and studying plays and moves of some of the senior athletes, and still he wasn't even able to make the first cut in tenth grade.

He convinced himself that he just needed more determination, and that if he was persistent enough, anything was possible. So before eleventh grade he solicited the help from a recent graduate who was one of the stars of our recent state championship team. The experienced player agreed to work with him, day in and day out, all summer long. All of the young player's concentration went into learning the skills and techniques required to at least make the team, even if it meant only sitting on the bench as a third string guard.

Finally, for the first time in more than five years, he not only made the first cut, but even the last one. He was in sports heaven and ecstatic about being on the team as they played at all the other schools in our district for the pre-season scrimmages. The night before our first league game, the same night they would hand out the team's uniforms, and the day before his first chance to play in a gym full of spirited fans, the coach quietly mentioned that he had to let three more players go .... and he was one of them.

Well, that kid who so desperately wanted to play was me, and the next few days at school were exceptionally humiliating. There was pressure to not feel inadequate about everything I did and I couldn't gather the poise to watch my teammates play in the first few games. But seeing such disappointment in my character, Coach Leach pulled me aside to offer some valuable advice. "You know... you can hold your own with the players on the team, but they can't entertain an audience on stage the way you do," he advised. "Think about playing to your strengths."

That became a very pivotal moment in my life, when I realized that it might be more prudent to laser at least some of my attention on the things that came to me more naturally. I think my coach was happier than anyone to see me do well in the all school talent show the following year. I kept my love for sports, and even expanded my involvement in them, but also revitalized my interests in healthcare and performing illusions... investing in my strengths.

Adversity introduces a man to himself.

By searching internally to determine what attributes I could use to my advantage at that given moment in time, I was able to build on them over the years to come. As an avocation I delved into designing new types of illusions with a completely different spin from what audiences had experienced before.

I also began to hit the books fairly hard, knowing that pursuing an interest in optometry meant entering a very competitive field. Any hopes of being accepted into graduate school required a better grade point average than I currently had. Even at a young age, it seemed obvious that healthcare was becoming more commercialized over time. My ambitious goal involved developing a way to offer patients a more personalized experience than they had ever received before. I wanted them to feel a strong sense of sincerity from everyone within the practice.

A new challenge to myself became setting the stage to help improve people's lives, both through one-to-one contact within healthcare, as well as in a larger environment through the escapism of entertainment. What I came to realize is that it wasn't only changing my perception that made a difference; the timing of my decisions were equally as important. I am fortunate for keeping an open mind about change at the time I did.

On occasion, take a moment to step back and look in a mirror. Reevaluate whether or not you are using all of your strengths effectively. Imagine having to start from scratch, with absolutely nothing. What is the fastest way that you can attain your own meaningful description of success?

CHAPTER FIVE

A LACK OF SUPER VISION

Basic Ingredients

What is the justification that two people can look at the exact same picture and yet describe it completely differently? How is this possible? How can we be so unaware and not recognize that our preconceived notions and previous experiences are tainting the way we perceive things?

I remember stopping at a local convenience store on a Columbus Day weekend, the busiest tourism season for Lancaster County. I overheard a person from New York City (based on his accent) complaining to the clerk at the counter about the boredom he was anticipating for the next few days. "I can't believe I'm stuck here with my wife for the entire weekend," he said. "Not only is there very little to do out here in the country, but it seems that everything closes by eleven o'clock… there's no night life like 'the city.' We haven't seen the kind of shopping we have on Fifth Avenue and the Amish buggies are so slow that they're a road hazard. Is this what I left the city for?"

"Well," said the clerk, "You're right. That's pretty much what you'll find here." The visitor spun around unimpressed as he exited toward his vehicle.

Then, before I was able to reach the counter to pay for my items, another man entered the store, picked up a sandwich to purchase, and while paying the same cashier commented, "Wow, this sure beats my hectic life at home." (Again, his accent resonated from the Big Apple) "Your countryside is so beautiful, and I love all the quaint little shops. Without all the noise from the city, I'll probably sleep better than I have in years. Is it always like this around here?"

"Well," said the clerk, "You're right. That's pretty much what you'll find here."

I had been fortunate to overhear a very thought-provoking lesson for understanding how we tend to find exactly what we're looking for. When we have specific expectations, our perception amazingly guides us toward them and magnifies whatever we hope to see.

Despite our ability to scan an enormous amount of visual information all at once, our focus can bypass many other things plainly within our view. It's as if they remain invisible. How many times have you witnessed a couple in a restaurant that is evidently deeply in love, as they are completely oblivious to anything else in the room? They only have eyes for each other.

When we're so preoccupied with what's directly in front of us, we fail to recognize certain aspects of our surroundings... alternative ways to evaluate what we could be taking for granted.

Here's an exercise that was given to me during an art class in elementary school which may teach you something about yourself and the way your own mind is inclined to work. Ideally you will need a dozen three inch by five inch index cards (otherwise you can use a piece of paper and draw a dozen rectangles on it, like the one in the figure below). Keep in mind, if you don't actually try this before reading through the following pages, you'll lose the chance to discover something interesting about yourself... and we have so few opportunities to learn something so profound.

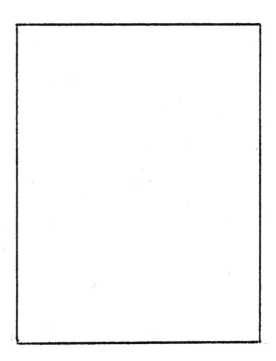

Using a pen or pencil, divide the first card (or drawn rectangle) into four equal compartments. They should be fairly precise, so that if you were to cut out the pieces they would be interchangeable (which is what my art teacher required us to do). You will most likely have a drawing similar to the next figure.

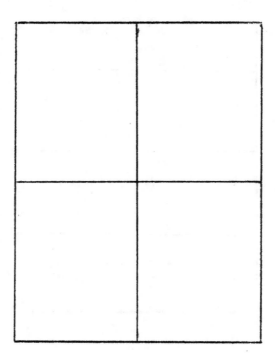

However... there's another way that you could have divided the rectangle into four exactly equal compartments. Take a moment to see if you can come up with an alternative method before you turn the page to look at the next figure.

Either one of these examples also accomplishes the same requirements for creating four exactly equal compartments.

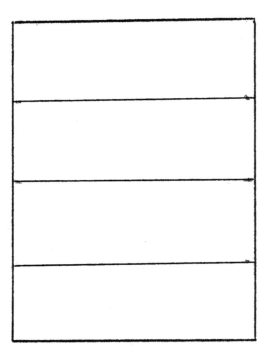

Believe it or not, there is actually another way in which the same requirements can be met. Give this some adequate thought before rushing to turn the page.

As you can see, there are an infinite number of ways to create the four equal compartments, limited only by our own imagination.

Initially we can only see what we've traditionally witnessed in the past. Then once we realize that after dividing the rectangle in half, it's a mere task of creating equal mirror images, we find that our options are truly infinite.

As with most undertakings and challenges in front of us, at the onset we may only see the single narrow path most familiar to us. If we are willing to broaden our perspective, there are usually abundant possibilities for solving any equation.

As referenced earlier, the key to stimulating your creativity and modifying your perspective is to interrupt your pattern of thinking. Sometimes the least bit of leverage can trip ingrained thought patterns that normally would be difficult to alter. If someone instructed you to *not* look at anything red in the room, it would be impossible to do that. In fact, you would suddenly notice that everything red in the room was almost popping out at you.

Ideas come from seeing the same thing as everyone else but thinking something different.

The quickest way to change our perspective about someone else is to place ourselves in his or her shoes. Most of us have no concept of how to actually do that. Just like an actor, it requires totally immersing ourselves into the physical and emotional mindset of another individual... to feel the same pressures, temperament, and predicaments to which the other person is exposed to. For most people, this is a very difficult thing to do.

Many less fortunate and poverty stricken individuals often voice that politicians are detached from reality, and until they stand in the same long lines for food stamps or sleep on the same old worn out mattresses, they will never quite relate to another person's suffering. It's far too easy for anyone to look at pictures of tragedies on television or in a magazine and only be sympathetic in the moment. Until we literally place ourselves in someone else's physical environment, we will never comprehend what they deal with on a day-to-day basis.

A lasting impression was made on me while visiting a small, remote village on the outskirts of Port au Prince in Haiti. As part of a voluntary medical team, we came upon a town that had been nicknamed "Carton." Its name was derived by the fact that most of the children were orphans and lived in cardboard boxes on the streets. Without the comforts of a home, security, or acceptable means of hygiene, they scampered through garbage cans day to day hoping to find any form of discarded food or liquids to help them sustain their neglected lives.

Until I actually walked the streets right next to them, it was impossible to relate to such deplorable conditions. As the torrential rains began, they would all run for cover in the nearest corrugated box they could find. They used these same measly containers in the evening as an emotional barrier from the active gunfire that took place on the streets.

Nearby, I ventured into one of Mother Teresa's projects designated for all of the newly born homeless children. What I found were rows and rows of small metal cribs that were sometimes even shared by more than one infant. The room felt more like a kennel for animals, as many of the children had dried mucous and feces splattered across their bodies, not to mention the insects that found their smell appealing.

I noticed two large containers of water on the side of the room, one marked "tops" and the other labeled "bottoms." When I inquired as to what they were used for, they explained that the first was use to bathe the top halves of the children once a day, and the other was used for the bottom halves. We were also advised that if we wanted to offer any assistance we could be most helpful by simply touching the children's skin. A large number of them would die due to a mere lack of human contact, as there were too few people to care for the growing number of abandoned babies.

Some of what we experience in life creates an impact that never leaves us. All of our past exposures affect our capacity to retain new information and the speed in which we learn. There are four primary levels of awareness for most of our experiences. First, people don't know that they don't know. Second, they know they don't know. Third, they don't know they know. And finally, they know they know. For example, I enjoyed playing tennis for many years without ever taking a lesson. During those years I became much more competitive but didn't develop a stronger game as quickly had I been guided by a professional instructor.

When I would play against someone more adept at disguising the spin on the ball, he would have a distinct advantage. I would beat myself up not knowing why I wasn't returning more shots. I would try to justify that I was just having a bad day rather than understanding why my opponent was winning more points.

Later, I began to question whether my opponent was using a technique I might not be aware of... a strategy that was giving him a competitive edge. Maybe there was something I needed to improve upon that was stagnating and preventing me from advancing to the next level. Eventually, in scrutinizing his swing preparation, I realized that the other player did know something unfamiliar to me, and he was genuinely using it to his advantage.

In time, by mimicking his specific motions and timing, I was able to translate and imitate my opponent's strokes and begin to experiment with the benefits of using his modified swing. It would take weeks to develop a feel for these new mechanics, but before long they would almost become natural. Suddenly, and without any cognitive awareness, I found myself subliminally using the same stroke to my advantage, too. In many aspects of life, our learning process travels through each of these phases before recognizing a certainty of accomplishment.

Before leaving this chapter, try cutting a three by five index card into four exactly equal pieces other than any of the configurations that were shown above. Then try it two more times using completely different patterns. When you do something *physically* it creates a much stronger impact than just merely reading about it. This is the first "step" to truly putting yourself into someone else's shoes.

Prescription to Start

One of the biggest pitfalls we face in not being able to progress more speedily is that we are, innately, creatures of habit. We can be very reluctant and even forcibly oppose having to leave our well-established comfort zones. When we approach a risk of anything too foreign to us, our resistance can undeniably inhibit our growth.

An important talent and methodology for acting is to understand how to re-act. But when confronted with personal challenges, if the only thing we can do is react, we are already too late. We need to make better use of our mind's eye and alter the way we see the world around us as it continues to transform ever faster.

Winners are usually the ones who are quicker to take the first step.

About ninety-eight percent of the population falls into the category of being reactive. They simply respond to events that have already taken place. Only one percent are in stealth mode. These are the active people, always on the cutting edge, and committed to making things happen. And finally, there's another one percent who don't have a clue that anything's ever happening. They're caught up in their own little world, unaware that we live in a different culture than we did ten years ago.

It is the trail of the first one percent that we should try to emulate and where we should concentrate our focus. And, very unexpectedly, it often takes less energy to act than it does to react. In knowing how to change our perception and by modifying where we choose to look, we can learn to accomplish so much more using even less effort. Working smarter rather than harder affords us obvious rewards.

One definition of insanity is "continuing to do something the exact same way while expecting different results." If we persist in approaching life in the same way that we always have in the past, how can we expect to achieve a new outcome?

As a child we love to mimic our parents. Just place a set of keys in the hand of an infant and suddenly every hole has the potential to be a lock. Give an older child a measuring tape and they will sometimes begin sizing up everything in sight. Instantly they are intrigued and want to know the comparative size of everything feasible for them to measure.

Strasburg is a well known tourist destination in Lancaster, PA. It is home to a huge train museum. Children are often fascinated with trains and even the tracks they must ride on. If they become curious enough to measure the distance between tracks, they'll find that they're exactly four feet, eight and a half inches apart. What an odd configuration—and who came up with such a random size for such an expansive network of rails that cover our entire continent? Why wasn't it four and a half feet or simply five feet? Well, the early expatriate settlers of our country modeled their new railroad system here after the British railroads, which also had the exact same distance between them. So why were those tracks exactly four feet, eight and a half inches apart?

The British railroads were actually modeled after the early tram rails that were used in the larger cities at the time. It turns out that they were based on the width of the axles of the earlier horse-drawn wagons, because these wheels had to match the previous ruts in the road for fear of breaking the wagon. So where did those original ruts come from?

Well, we need to go back even further, because they were based on the ruts left behind from the war chariots of Imperial Rome, more than two thousand years ago. This peculiar measurement was derived from the average width of a harness to accommodate the hindquarters of two average size horses. And this measurement just happened to be four feet, eight and a half inches.

So essentially, it was the rear ends of two horses that were used to create the very measurements that exist in our modern railway system today. But, it doesn't end there.

When the United States sends a space shuttle into orbit, it has auxiliary boosters attached to the side of the fuel tank known as solid rocket boosters. Our space program purchases them from the engineers at Thiokol in Utah, who would prefer to make them even larger. The problem is that they have to be transported by train, which means traveling east through the Rocky Mountains. There are several tunnels that the trains must go through that are not much larger than the tracks, which you know are only four feet, eight and a half inches apart. So in essence, the early days of the Romans are limiting our futuristic NASA space program! The most advanced technology in the world is "stuck in a rut" because its rocket power is not based on horsepower; it's based on a horse's ass.

Again, this counter productive drawback in not being able to grow more steadily is that we are inherently creatures of habit. Too often the concept of something alien to us is enough to place us into an overly cautious mode of stagnancy. Even if we're on the "right track" we'll get run over if we just sit there. The reason why some people have an easier time breaking out of this shell is that they're not reluctant to engage their imagination.

Your easiest advantage is to simply dream more than others.

For our imagination to work effectively, we must purposefully try varying the behavior patterns of our past and maneuver away from our established comfort zones. This is true for individuals, and equally true for entire companies. If you look at the top one hundred companies on the Fortune 500 list, there are very few left compared to the list from thirty years ago.

One example of a company that fell off track but is hoping to gradually regain a segment of its previous market share is Kodak. Not long ago Kodak almost completely dominated the camera film industry. Its branding was powerful which paved the way for near exclusivity. Then we experienced the advent of digital cameras along with digital processing which rocketed the industry out of control, not unlike what digital media did to every other previous form of video and audio recording. Kodak didn't see the magnitude of such a gigantic wave in its path and was resting too heavily on its niche film market. By the time they began to recognize the severity of the shift in consumer products, it was too late. Since then, they have managed to refocus on their once highly regarded name as experts in other areas of their industry and are back in the arena again. But now they are treading water with many other swimmers.

Albert Einstein once said that you cannot solve a problem with the same consciousness that caused it. His implication was that we must constantly step away from our imbedded mindset. He was also emphatic in his belief we can further broaden our customary thought process by establishing a team of trusted friends who equally welcome innovative thinking. The more we surround ourselves with open minds, the more likelihood that one or more new perspectives will develop into valuable ideas.

A commonly echoed saying in business states "it's amazing how much a team of people can accomplish when they stop caring about whom gets the credit." Brainstorming with like-minded people will often create a synergistic environment that is inclined to perpetuate itself.

When looking for an entertaining illustration to promote the concept of team collaboration and make sure everyone is on the same page, here is something I've used for many businesses. It has proven to be a captivating opener for bringing symmetry to a group.

Have each person in the room write down a single digit number from one to nine. Next to that, have them write a second and different digit than the first, and then a third and also dissimilar digit next to that one.

Each person in the room will have their own unique, three-digit number. At this point, have them reverse these three digits to create a new number, and then subtract the smaller three digit number from the larger one. This will generate a new three-digit number, or in a few cases, a two-digit number. (If someone is left with only a two-digit number, have the person add a zero to either the front or back of the two digits to help maintain a consistency among the group.)

Next have them reverse their new number and then add these last two three-digit numbers together. Rather astonishingly, everyone in the room will end up with the exact same number... "1,089." You can now either reveal your previously written prediction (hidden from everyone's view until now) of 1089, or else begin asking individuals to reveal their total as they discover that they each share precisely the same answer.

This is just an entertaining way to establish that even though each of us is unique, we still share a common bond with each other. (An alternative method for selecting the original numbers that is even more intriguing is to choose one digit from their phone number, another from their social security number, and the third one from a secret "pin" number. This insinuates that each number is individually personalized, with more of an emotional attachment to it.

Since you now know how to arrive at the specific number above, you can probably surmise how it's possible to customize the final answer, simply by adding another calculation or two. Try formulating an additional step to the equation above that will personalize your presentation with a more relevant answer.

Warning Label

By not looking beyond how we operate most comfortably, we can develop unwanted and controlling habits very quickly. Take tennis for an example. I was having far too much fun simply playing and competing rather than taking a lesson for fear it would feel regimented and somewhat like work. I was too focused on spending quality time with my friends and getting exercise than to take more time out of my week for developing improved techniques. Unfortunately, when I finally did decide that it was time to take a few lessons and improve my game, it was even harder to break my old bad habits than it was to develop new skills.

The polar opposite scenario happened when a nearby neighbor, who was also a police officer, convinced me to take a gun safety course he was teaching. Since I had very little knowledge about guns, I decided that any advice I receive, especially about something so alien to me, might prove itself worthy as another form of education.

In hindsight, I acquired a more important lesson than the value of gun safety. Because I knew very little about shooting, I was extremely focused on every learning aspect of the class, and especially alert to the potential dangers regarding poor gun handling. Interestingly, because I had no prior experience or opportunity to develop any poor shooting habits, I became the most accurate marksman in the class and received a first place trophy... not for being the most improved shooter, but for being the best shooter.

To this day, I still have little interest in shooting, but because I entered the class with an unbiased frame of mind and had no wrong habits to break, I was also the easiest one in the class to teach.

Repetition is the mother skill, though it can actually work for us or against us. When we develop particular mechanics or do certain things so repetitively that they become second nature, we are often completely unaware of the *way* we do them. Many of our actions, and even reactions, become instinctual, without ever a thought as to how we're functioning within our routine.

Tom Amberry knew this all too well as a recreational basketball enthusiast. Even in his eighties, after retiring from podiatry, he would often sink more than five hundred consecutive baskets from the free throw line. In fact, one winter he made two thousand seven hundred and fifty shots in a row! He definitely understood the meaning of removing all negative thoughts and being in the moment.

A classic example of not being in the moment occurs while driving a car. We may drive for extended periods of time, all the while making subconscious decisions, as we daydream, get caught up in the scenery, or listen to music or an audio book. The lure of multi-tasking has us constantly trying to be more productive. Whenever we relinquish part of our focus and attentiveness in one area there's a trade off, and we must surrender the prospective of gaining adequate information from more than one place.

We never have to peel the onion skin back very far before seeing examples of how an intensity of focus can dramatically alter a life. There were two young girls growing up in my neighborhood who at one point were particularly appreciative of all the attention they received, since they were both legally blind. As their mother consistently encouraged them not to rely on sympathy they each chose to immerse themselves in a mainstream education.

The girls began using laptops with Braille keyboards to take notes in all their classes in an effort to keep up with their peers. Not only did they make it through the many physical and emotional hurdles of high school, but they each graduated from college with double majors, Shelly from Immaculata College (with degrees in history and music) and Jennifer from California State (with degrees in business and special education).

Think back and identify at least one instance that personally inspired you when someone you know was able to overcome their adversities. What have you approached with an open mind? What was the outcome? A small change in our perception can provide traction for discovering how ideas about vision become visionary ideas.

Adult Dosage

As children we once had endless imaginations. A simple bed sheet drawn between two chairs instantly transforms into a tent. A grove of backyard trees becomes an enchanted forest. Increasing age tempts us to dream far less often. We begin asking fewer questions, become much more accepting, and make too many assumptions. In order to interrupt these detrimental patterns for creativity, we need to look for and become more aware of important triggers. Our imagination comes to life when we can visualize ourselves on an endless journey, open to anything in our path that will lift our expectations beyond traditional thinking.

Not long ago one of my patients brought her young child into the exam room with her while I was examining her eyes. She tried to keep him occupied with a coloring book, but then reprimanded him for coloring outside the lines. While I understood her mode of thinking, she was unknowingly training her child not to think on his own. Someone else had created the guidelines for his picture, and possibly the child's imagination envisioned something more creative, beyond the confines of the original concept. By restricting his own impression for the drawing, the parent may have also reduced the child's initiative to think independently.

When you purchase the latest phase of electronic gadgetry or a new type of software, are you compelled to go straight to the instructions? I have several friends who always insist on "playing" with something new, even for a prolonged time, to see what they can first learn on their own. It is during this precious time (which can never be duplicated again), before reading the instructions, that they sometimes discover an offbeat function or alternative use for it that would have otherwise never been discovered.

Giving in to the anxiousness of wanting to use a new purchase (which is the ninety-eight percent of followers referred to earlier) it's possible to ruin an opportunity for revealing our own creativity and our own instincts for learning. The directions will always be there if and when we need them.

Our minds only work to their full capacity when they are completely open.

This is the same reason why most children under twelve are savvier on a computer than someone five times their age. They've had the luxury of free time to simply play and explore, and uncover its infinite capabilities. This is preferable preparation for them education-ally as they delve into a thinking process that can reward them later for their ability to see things differently. Some of the most creative ideas come from beginners, not experts.

More than a hundred years ago, a man came home from work one evening only to discover his wife deathly ill. He tried to comfort her and attempted cooling her feverish sweats, but nothing he could do would relieve her severe abdominal pain. As there was no modern transportation available at that time, the man began running through his neighborhood in hopes of summoning an available doctor.

He eventually returned with one, only to learn that his wife was suffering from acute appendicitis. The doctor announced that in order to save her life, she would require immediate surgery.

Surgery in a patient's home was actually more common in that day, although at this time of the evening, the only lighting available was very poor. The physician insisted it wasn't enough to help him see for the seriousness of the procedure. The man had only a couple lanterns, which were almost insignificant in the dimly lit room. He thought for a moment, and then began running throughout his home, gathering every candle available. But still, there was not adequate lighting.

Again, he contemplated, and then suddenly began scurrying, once more, this time grabbing all the mirrors he could possibly find. Interestingly, the mirrors reflected the candlelight back and forth innumerable times, creating such a brilliantly lit room that the doctor was able to do the surgery and save the woman's life. This event was most likely the trigger that encouraged this same man to develop the very first incandescent bulb as his name was Thomas Edison.

Another life-changing trigger occurred while a man named Joe Woodland was vacationing on a beach. His mind was far removed from business, yet as he sat in his beach chair casually stroking his fingers through the sand, he noticed something intriguing. With each stroke of his fingers, he found that it was impossible to create the exact same pattern as the previous one. Nature seemed to be suggesting that there were an infinite number of designs that could be formed with his little finger troughs.

After sitting back and contemplating the significance of the endless number of configurations possible, he was struck with a revolutionary concept. This was the trigger that led him to develop the bar coding system present on almost every item available for purchase in the world. Ultimately, his simple concept made one of the most influential improvements ever for customer service, inventory control, speed of delivery, and reduced record keeping.

There are many invisible triggers that are nudging at us everyday. The challenge is in being able to identify what they are and then having the initiative to act on them. So what's the secret to being able to find these triggers, and where do we begin to look for them?

The best way to inspire ourselves to look for new triggers is to begin to expect the unexpected. As mentioned earlier, we have a remarkable and natural tendency to find what we're looking for, as long as we consciously remain open-minded. The more difficult task is in letting go of our old ideas. With practice it becomes easier to disassociate ourselves from the familiar and recognize some of the, once invisible, triggers right in front of us.

A nearby friend, who was known as Charlie "Tremendous" Jones, had always advised me that the most influential differences in our lives will come from the books we read and the people we meet. It's much too easy to treat what we read, and especially the people we come into contact with, too casually and without pausing to ponder their significance. It's very possible that any one person or paragraph, at any given moment, can substantially affect our lives... yet we disregard their potential which, therefore, prevents if from ever happening.

After living near Hollywood and sharing conversations with various screen artists, I came up with a simple trigger for illustrating our restrictive imagination. During a meeting, I sometimes take a moment to have everyone draw his or her own impression of what an alien from another galaxy might look like. Each person should conceptualize a very mobile but previously unseen creature. (Because I use the word "mobile," people subliminally infer that this alien must somehow be able to sense its surroundings.) To this day I have never met anyone who didn't insist on drawing at least one or two eyes, or possibly several eyes, as a way for their alien to see. Just because *we* require eyes for our vision, our primary source of acquiring information, we easily become locked into that mindset. There are even creatures on our own planet that must rely on ground vibrations, sonar, or smell instead of vision for their survival.

When given absolutely no rules, boundaries, restrictions, or conditions whatsoever, we need to practice releasing our imagination to its fullest extent and not rely on the Hollywood of yesterday and what we've been exposed to in the past.

**A smart man knows
the rules, but a
wiser man knows
the exceptions.**

The majority of our limits are self-imposed and detrimental by sacrificing our true ability to see. These artificial boundaries are nothing more than a distorted belief system, which means that it's possible to change our perception in one breath. We can consciously alter the way we feel by simply adjusting our attitude. Sometimes even a minor physiological change, such as smiling (which induces the release of endorphins, responsible for our feeling of contentment), is enough to refresh us and adjust our outlook. This simple act requires much less energy than anger and can stimulate our entire nervous system in a positive way.

If a picture is worth a thousand words, a noteworthy exercise is to draw a large box in the middle of a page and write down seven or eight distinguishing traits that you feel are a true representation of yourself. They can be good or bad ones, but try to be brutally honest. Alternatively, you can have someone else write down what characteristics they see in you, too. Another individual will be less biased emotionally and provide you with a clearer portrait of what other people see in you.

Now, outside the box, surround it by writing down seven or eight different traits that you would *like* to have, or ones for which you would at least hope to strive. When finished, this diagram will depict a simplified version of what is already yours and how easily you can break through a thin shell in any direction of your choice. Much in the way that someone dieting might post a picture of an obese person on their refrigerator, as a constant reminder of better eating habits, having this illustration allows you to be consistently aware of making a simple behavior modification. A picture provides instant recognition of how you can now grow and diversify in many directions at once.

A more dramatic exercise is to take a three-by-five index card and tear a small hole in it just large enough to put your finger through it. Now, tear the hole even bigger so that it's now large enough to put your whole hand through it. Finally, make one last tear, but this time make it sizeable enough that you can put your whole head through it.

At first this will seem irrationally impossible, as the card you're holding is only three inches by five inches, and your head has a circumference of approximately twenty-three inches. Aren't you limited by the boundary of the card's edge, since the perimeter is a fixed measurement? Well, that's the catch. Your mind tells you, from previous experiences, that you can't change the parameters of something that already has a predetermined size. When, in reality, you can change the size of the perimeter by changing your perspective.

If you go back and look at the drawing of the maze on page 83, you will notice if you make the exact same tears on your index card as each line depicted in the diagram, you will be lengthening its edge and increasing its capacity to expand. Duplicate the example and try it for yourself. Now your head will truly fit through the hole quite easily. In fact, by using a scissors and carefully increasing the number of cuts you make, using the same format as in the drawing, you will be able to actually cut a hole large enough that you can walk through it standing up.

Again, our mind glances at the perimeter of the card and quickly assumes that the edge is a fixed entity with no feasible way to stretch its boundary. Take a moment to look around at your immediate surroundings. Can you determine what self imposed limits are subconsciously overshadowing your thinking and stifling your creativity?

CHAPTER SIX:
OPTICAL DELUSIONS

Seeing the Invisible

Numerous studies in neuroscience tell us that all top performers share a common practice in achieving their success. That shared facet for reaching their goals is known as "visualization."

Recent research has demonstrated in several trial tests that when we measure the brain's neural activity, as far as visual imagery, our mind creates a picture of an object the same way whether we are actually seeing it with our eyes open or just imagining it with our eyes closed. This finding has dramatic implications in making visualization a very powerful tool for helping us to achieve our goals. Most successful actors, athletes, inventors, and entrepreneurs have mastered this technique. Each of them likely shares a natural instinct to visualize "what they want to happen." The stronger their visualization is, the more capable they are of bringing their thoughts to fruition.

The best way to predict the future is to create it.

A critical advantage that someone brings to the table in using visualization is they have already trained their imagination to be more active. Occasionally it's helpful to purposely let our minds drift away as we search for inspiration. But in time, we need to transform those bits of information into something more tangible to see where it will take us.

This picture consists of little more than eight (partial) spots. Can you visualize what they create? It's invisible... and yet it seems very real.

Visualization can be the best form of rehearsal in preparation for a stressful challenge. A professional athlete cannot afford to choke when competing, especially during a championship event. In the boardroom, a simple oversight during a sales presentation could be very costly when a potential buyer has to make a comparative decision.

Major James Nesmeth comes to mind as someone who relied on his own strong sense of visualization not only to protect his sanity, but also to save his life. While fighting for our country in North Vietnam, he was captured and taken prisoner. He was locked in a small cage, not even tall enough for him to stand erect. A prisoner of war, he was kept there for more than seven years. During all those years, which must have felt like eternity, there was never a moment when he could fully extend his entire body at the same time. In his hunched over state, he developed a variety of exercises in an attempt to maintain muscle tone and to keep his body from withering away.

His interminable daydreaming would often take him back to his favorite golf course, which probably seemed like a lifetime ago. Each day, in distinctly recalling each fairway, he would imagine his swing, the rise of the ball, how distant it would fly, and the judgment necessary for the next optimal stroke. He envisioned each hole and practiced it with such emotional depth that it almost became physical. Almost as an attempt to preserve his idle brain cells, he would play the whole course in his mind, even though he hadn't touched a golf club in more than half a decade.

Finally, after seven years of atrociously restricted captivity, caged like an animal, he was released and sent back to the States. His health had greatly deteriorated, and he required weeks of evaluations, both physically and mentally, in an effort to bring his body back to its pre-existing condition. Eventually he returned to the golf course that for so long had been only a mental image; he hadn't witnessed its actual beauty in years.

Formerly, being the golf fanatic that he was, he had kept detailed statistics of every hole he'd ever played. He had made notes about his good strokes, the bad ones, and any mistakes he made or corrections he attempted, always striving to tweak his game.

The first time he stepped back on the course again, after all his rehabilitation and ready to record his every stroke, he shot the lowest round that he'd ever played in his life. He knocked "twenty strokes" off his game. His ability to visualize and work on his game mentally during all those years had become a reality... possibly no different had he been playing on the course itself.

Most people are fairly adept at closing their eyes to envision something unfortunate happening, such as making a poor impression with a new acquaintance, or the embarrassment of a less than average performance, especially in public. How often do we contemplate a mental image of something that could go even *better* than expected, rather than worrying about the chance for failure? This same guided imagery is what assists many patients in getting through a dental procedure or chemotherapy treatments.

Look the Other Way

My interest in illusions was spurred in first grade during the school's family talent show. An older student began linking and unlinking solid steel rings almost at will, as if they were miraculously able to melt right through each other. I was totally mesmerized, not because I believed it was actually possible, but because his effortlessness made it appear so real. I became infatuated about learning the secret behind his demonstration. When I saw the very same illusion advertised in the back of a magazine, all of my birthday and Christmas savings were immediately in the mail.

When my long awaited package finally arrived, I was so disappointed and bitter due to the simplicity of the secret that I threw the rings in a drawer and didn't touch them for months. Then, almost a year later, I saw another magician perform the same illusion on television. I watched him very closely and was completely fooled again, as my rings didn't seem to work the same way... it must be a different illusion.

The magic of life makes its appearance when we're willing to look beyond what we've always seen in the past.

I hesitatingly went back to my drawer to rediscover my own set, and, for the first time, began to appreciate there was a lot more to creating this deceptive illusion than merely understanding the secret itself. I always knew that simply owning a piano did not necessarily make someone a pianist. I soon learned that to present this illusion correctly would require more months of diligent practice than I ever anticipated. More than that, I had to master how to perform it backwards... exactly opposite from my point of view.

For this illusion to be effective, the perception of the audience had to be distorted from my reality. My perspective of what I was doing was complicated, very detail oriented, and required a lot of dexterity. At the same time, I had to appear very nonchalant and matter of fact, and give the impression that nothing special or difficult was happening. It was paramount to take the audience's perspective into account. I found the best way to practice was in front of a mirror, so that I could see exactly what they would be watching. However, I had to simultaneously learn how to ignore what I saw because I wouldn't have the mirror as a crutch while actually performing. I knew it also had to feel believable in my own mind for the illusion to seem real to the audience.

For instance, if I wanted to create the impression that I had something in my hand when indeed I didn't, I not only had to imagine, very intently, that it was there, but I also had to invisibly *feel* the size, weight, and texture in my mind if I was going to be convincing to anyone else. My entire demeanor and physical awareness had to accurately replicate the essence that something really was in my hand. This also served as an impressionable lesson for placing myself into someone else's shoes.

I recall learning of an unconventional business perspective as one of my college buddies was attempting to grow his new business. He explained to me that he had just hired a chauffer. I could barely hold back my smirk as I inquired, "Okay, and who are we trying to impress? Image is one thing, but wouldn't it be more cost effective to just drive like the rest of us? Isn't that a little decadent for just getting starting?"

When he revealed his rationale to me, suddenly I became very intrigued, as it made a lot of sense. He clarified that since much of his time and energy was wasted in heavy traffic, he had hired someone at minimum wage to do all his driving. The driver's obligation was to not chitchat and distract my friend from his work, but to strictly focus on where he was going. My friend, in turn, was able to make numerous uninterrupted phone calls, take full advantage of his laptop, and make superior use of his time by having a mobile office in the backseat of his car. What initially appeared to be a frivolous expense turned out to be a brilliant business decision.

While attending Penn State, we had always darted between buildings using our own custom-made paths (knowing the fastest walk is a straight line) whenever we were late for class. Almost every student would cut through lawns and tightly around shrubbery while disregarding the intended use of the concrete walkways. It wouldn't take long before we had worn our own paths with direct routes to class that were much more efficient.

Rather than engage in a confrontation with the students and enforce them to use the designated walkways, the administration took an opposite approach. They decided that whenever new buildings were introduced to the campus, they would wait several months for the students to form their own paths before pouring any concrete. Only then would they make these same paths permanent. This ultimately allowed the students to create their own unique landscaping aesthetics as well as the most direct routes to their classes. This time and cost efficiency was still another lesson in having new eyes for the same landscape.

In attempting to improve my skills as an illusionist, I was fortunate to cross paths with a most celebrated person from the Netherlands. While attending a magicians' convention in England, many people could be overheard talking about this intriguing and soft-spoken gentleman who typified the quintessential grandfather. In trying to understand his quiet notoriety, I learned that Henk Vermeyden was the master instructor behind some of the most respected European entertainers. Many hopefuls from around the globe had come seeking the opportunity to work with him. And so, as another young and naïve visitor, I decided that should be my goal, too. I became exceptionally focused on trying to gain his attention as I realized his guidance might offer the most beneficial direction for improving my avocation.

The next several months I began an endless campaign of sending him every practice video, performance philosophy, and creative work in progress I could possibly compile. As much as I would have liked to place an overseas phone call to him, international calls were very expensive at the time, and I reasoned it would have taken countless attempts to reach someone so high profile. Instead I also sent him audio messages that discussed what I was currently working on and how grateful I would be for his help.

Finally, after nine very long months, he responded to me by mail. Then after a continuing duration of propaganda on my part, he finally relented into taking me on as a short-term student. I was ecstatic, convinced that this was the golden seal of approval I desperately needed for taking my performances to the next level. I made immediate arrangements to go abroad and work with him at his famous studio in the heart of Amsterdam.

Even though my short jaunt began with all the excitement one encompasses on an international journey, it ultimately became a disappointing venture which left me feeling empty. I had been certain that I would return with all of the knowledge, savvy, and confidence of his other students. Instead, it made me appreciate that the real creativity I was probing for had to somehow come from within me... especially if I truly wanted to express the type of artistry I had envisioned. Eventually I realized that my experience had taught me the value in trusting my own perspective. While my instructor really had been helpful, what his accomplished students had in common was the tenacity to dig deeper inside themselves.

I resolved to the fact that the finest ideas may be much closer to home if I was willing to use my eyes differently. An insightful teacher, respected mentor, or even a trusted friend can be invaluable for helping us to see things from another vantage point. Equally important is daring to step beyond our established areas of comfort and trusting our intuitive choices.

Last year I found myself standing on the roof of the largest open volume structure in the world. Much larger than any enclosed sports arena is the NASA Vehicle Assembly Building, the enormous indoor facility where the world's most advanced spacecrafts are assembled. From the myriad of quality control centers, to the diversity of engineers and adjunct personnel, to the sheer size of the space vessels and physical expanse of the grounds, to the costly commitment of our government stemming back to the Kennedy years, it is mind-boggling to witness all of the integrated events taking place on the morning of an actual launch. All of it culminates in an explosive ball of fire that takes a small room of passengers to a manmade station floating somewhere in space.

The magnitude of the entire program was awe-inspiring, to say the least. But I couldn't help but reflect back to a man who has long been forgotten. His name was Joseph Kittinger, and without his courageous speculation that man could survive temperatures of almost one hundred degrees below zero and the near vacuum of space, none of our current day space program could have matured to its present state.

Try dreaming more often when you're awake.

During the embryonic stage of our space program back in 1960, this brave soul allowed his dreams to truly soar into new and unchartered territory, which provided an indispensable and groundbreaking perspective. Wearing a primitive pressurized suit, he risked his life by taking a helium balloon up into the atmosphere until it reached a height of 102,000 feet, just to discover if it was even possible for someone to survive at such an altitude. Then, armed with nothing more than a small oxygen tank and a parachute, he jumped out of the balloon's basket hoping that somehow his body would survive the journey back to earth again.

Battling considerable challenges from his ill-fitting armor, he still holds the record for the fastest traveling human being (with a speed of over 600 mph and almost breaking the sound barrier) without a spacecraft. His parachute eventually opened and landed him safely on the ground. If it hadn't been for this man's unsettling curiosity and persistence in knowing what might be possible, our space program may have never developed into what we celebrate today.

Some of the most inventive minds in the world became that way by their simple willingness to dream more often. The good news is that dreaming is free, relaxing, requires no education, takes very little effort, and is something anyone can do. So why don't we give it more precedence? What ideas have you explored from day dreaming?

An Opposite View

Even though we are generally accustomed to seeing things from a certain perspective out of habit, a very liberating exercise can be to look at something from the exact opposite point of view.

Several years ago Allen Fahden was seeking a dramatic way to promote his newly released book among the thousands of other books that are also released each month. Instead of following the typical protocol of placing it amid the immense competition at various book retailers, he took the exact opposite approach. Not only did he open his own bookstore, but this was about to become a bookstore like no one had ever seen. Sure, there were the typical sections for self-help, religion, sports, cooking, etc. There were also thousands of books in his inventory; except that none of them was different... they were *all* his book. His book was the only book you could purchase in every category.

It wasn't very long before the local media caught word on his innovative tactics and unusual retail venture. No matter how cautiously they covered this off-beat story, they knew his shenanigans were sure to capture a lot of attention. In very little time, the news spread to a national level, both on television and in print, because of the inimitability and wackiness of his store. Needless to say his book received a priceless amount of publicity, which further substantiated his premise for thinking the opposite way of everyone else.

On a more commonplace level, I am currently involved in a business partnership for some real estate investment properties. I sometimes overhear other landlords remark about how fortunate their tenants are that they've been provided a place to live, even though the tenants are contributing by paying a monthly rent. Occasionally a feeling of superiority swells around their conversations as they see themselves on a higher plane than their occupants.

In comparison, I personally try to look at this same scenario from an exact opposite point of view. I like to consider the tenants who are renting from us as employees. Rather than equipping them with computers, business tools, and office equipment, we are supplying them with refrigerators, washers, and dryers. It's as though each rental unit is a satellite office and each prospective tenant is a subcontractor who could generate an income for us (by paying their rent) while being responsible for micromanaging their individual location.

By viewing each tenant as a profitable employee who can help our business grow, not only does it change my perspective, but also my attitude in solving any problems (such as replacing worn out appliances or repainting a room) together as a team. For this reason, I typically have a favorable rapport with them and very few complaints or turnovers. In fact, many of them have rented from us for more than ten years.

I also stumbled upon an ideal example of opposite thinking recently while I was traveling and confronted with a frustrating layover at the Houston airport. My connecting flight had been cancelled, and I was having difficulty trying to rearrange another flight home that same evening. As I gazed at the flight schedule monitors looking for alternate possibilities, an elderly man driving one of the hallway transport vehicles came up behind me and waited. When I finally turned around, I found him staring back at me as he offered, "Can I help you to get somewhere?"

It was late in the day and I was exhausted from a long day of meetings. The last thing I needed was a ride down the corridor; I was still hoping to get home that night. "I don't think so... I need a little more than just a ride in your vehicle," I replied. "I'm working on a way to get home since my flight was cancelled, but thanks anyway." I figured he had fulfilled his obligation of being polite to a prospective customer, and now I could get back to my homework.

Instead he stated, "Well, my job is to help people get to where they want to go."

"Thanks, but I don't need a golf cart, I need another plane," I answered. Then he quickly responded, "Well, you're just not familiar with my job title. You see, I'm in the transportation business and my responsibility is to help people reach their final destination in any way I can, not just with this cart. I know all too well which flights are typically most available and reliable, and which personnel are most compassionate and more likely to accommodate your needs. So I can probably be of more service to you than any monitor."

Wow, my preemptive thinking had already prejudged and categorized this kind fellow long before I understood his likelihood of being able to help me. Not only did he use all his trivial knowledge to its greatest capacity, but he took great pride in his career and was an exemplary representative for his company. He was inevitably one of the most helpful people I had met all day.

Sometimes the premise of doing something completely opposite from what we know seems absurd. Imagine a restaurant giving away free meals to everyone who is dining there. It sure doesn't seem like a profitable game plan for a business that wants to survive, but I discovered a restaurant that welcomed this theory.

This restaurant traditionally had very few patrons during the early part of the week, so the owner came up with an intriguing solution for attracting people's attention. For many months he had been offering the local police and emergency crews free food while they were on duty, often several times a week. He saw it as a charitable gesture to the community and hoped that his thoughtfulness might spur an interest in others supporting his business. Unfortunately, his generosity was never appreciated enough to reciprocate for his losses.

Realizing that he was already giving away more than a dozen free meals a week, he decided to use the same number of them more to his advantage. He discontinued the free meals for the police and crew-members, and instead gave them away to the general public. Once a week, when it was least expected, he announced that everyone who was currently dining could leave without receiving a tab... every meal was "on the house." He was not incurring any more expense than he had before, but now word spread quickly. Suddenly everyone wanted to share in the mystery of who would receive a free dining experience.

Almost over night his business grew substantially, not to mention the extensive free press he also received. It wasn't so much about the concept of free food as it was the novelty of the idea... at any given moment the owner might be willing to make all the checks disappear.

> **Don't depend on what others see, learn to trust what you see.**

David Copperfield is still one of the highest paid and most respected names among illusionists. He has a permanent staff of more than thirty people who assist him in creating, building, and touring his shows year after year. His elaborate stage sets, sound and lighting systems, and large-scale illusions comprise one of the largest traveling productions of its kind.

Now contrast that with David Blaine, who began his rise to fame with nothing more than a couple handheld cameras and a deck of cards. As opposed to the grandeur of a Las Vegas showroom or some of the world's most prestigious stages, he meandered through local neighborhood streets focusing on people's reactions rather than the size of the props. He performed the same magical effects over and over while hunting for the most excitable responses that he could compile and pitch to a major network for television. Then, after knocking on dozens of doors, he eventually found a producer who picked up on the idea that there may be a market for selling people's reactions.

By taking the absolute opposite approach from what had always worked in the past, he rose to stardom within two television specials and David Blaine became a household name that is recognized everywhere on the planet.

There are many examples all around us of individuals taking an opposite approach to business than we'd normally expect. Probably the very first taste of business for the youngest of entrepreneurs was the old standby attempt at running a neighborhood lemonade stand. If you were really adventurous, you may have even extended your product line by selling pretzels along with your liquid refreshment.

A local woman from my community decided to try her luck with these exact same constituents, even though she began her venture much later in life. The only difference is that she added several choices of pretzel flavoring and a touch of her own branding. Apparently Anne Beiler must have found the perfect recipe because now her modest convenience stands, more than a thousand in number, can be found in almost every mall and airport across the globe. During a recent trip to Hong Kong, the very first sign I recognized after landing was Auntie Ann's Pretzels.

This same concept of opposite thinking can be applied to education, too. I remember a good friend of mine experiencing some trying moments while raising four teenagers. One particular evening, his son came home slightly inebriated after attending a party with his peers. Rather than yelling at him or losing his temper, which would have had little impact in his son's state, he very calmly invited the young man to join him in the living room for a relaxing chat. Before beginning their conversation, though, he had decided to record everything so that he'd be able to play it back for his son at a later time.

The next morning, while his son was still feeling what it meant to over imbibe, his father shared the recording with him so he could witness for himself the affects that alcohol had on him while answering questions. The recording made such an impression that his son became overly cautious about ever repeating the same antics again.

Some of my fondest memories for achieving the most from opposite thinking involved creating unique themes for events. When several of my college buddies wanted to throw a party and lure other students without resorting to a typical beer fest, they took a chance on offering an innovative free vacation.

They had found an inexpensive three-day "getaway for two" in the Bahamas, and had arranged for the trip to take place for some last minute travelers. They promoted it as a "Suitcase Party" in that one couple would win a free island vacation, but only under the condition that the winners had to leave straight from the party (they also supplied a waiting car for transportation to the airport). In other words, everyone attending the party had to come with their luggage packed and ready to leave, knowing that only one couple would actually win the surprise getaway.

Not only did they create a buzz that led to over four hundred people attending the party, but everyone was enthusiastic about contributing to the trip donation basket, which nearly paid for both the entire trip and the party itself.

Everyone who arrived came with suitcases packed and ready to leave. The luggage was stacked almost up to the ceiling around the entire perimeter of the room. There were golf clubs, tennis rackets, and everything imaginable for an island destination. To this day I don't think I've ever been to a drawing with such a heightened level of excitement, as each person had to pack everything they needed (right down to the sunscreen) in the event that he or she won. It was entertaining and comical to learn how many people had explained to their employers where they would be if they didn't show up for work that weekend.

While I wasn't the fortunate one to win the trip, I made use of reverse thinking as a joke while traveling with some friends at a later date. I had secretly purchased a ten-dollar Rolex knockoff while at one of the ports on a cruise. From a very short distance this watch was indistinguishable from its thirty-thousand-dollar namesake. The next day, while sitting among some of the more affluent guests on board, I suddenly acted "irritated" with my watch as I smacked the crystal several times.

"Darn Rolex," I said with an annoying tone of voice. "This thing's off by almost a minute, again." With that, I tore it off my wrist and flung it over the side of the ship. Completely stunned that I would nonchalantly throw away such an expensive timepiece, all the onlookers around me gazed in disbelief. It took every ounce of our composure for my friends and I to not burst out laughing.

When my partner and I wanted to thank our patients for their patronage to our practice, I devised an attention-getting message for inviting them to our event. Most of them were angry when they received a mailing from the United States Treasury shortly after tax day.

But not as much as when they read that they were being audited and had to appear in person... on a *weekend*.

Their blood pressure probably kept rising until they reached the last paragraph where they were instructed to come hungry and ready to have a good time. To this day, I wonder if any of the undeliverable mail was returned to the Treasury Department with employees curious about attending our event.

If we are willing to practice seeing things from an opposite point of view (even just as a diversion from your normal train of thought), it gradually becomes much easier to apply the same principles habitually... at a time of greater importance.

Room to Perceive

Sometimes our lives can be an endless string of meetings that eventually become a blur. The slightest injection of something unexpected can create a new freshness and awareness that can actually make our functions more worthwhile and memorable.

When given the opportunity, I will often schedule a meeting time for 10:07 a.m., 7:22 p.m., or using any other non-conforming number that stands out from the hour or half hour. A distinctive starting time automatically stands out on someone's schedule while equally encouraging them to be prompt. If the number also has significance (a birth date, numerical goal, etc.). . . all the better. When done repeatedly, attendees will often begin guessing the importance of the number before they even arrive. For this reason, I will occasionally give monetary gifts the same way. Instead of presenting someone with a hundred dollars, they're more likely to receive a check for a hundred and six dollars and forty-two cents with a note that justifies its meaning.

Rather than the typical refreshment breaks for longer meetings, I usually recommend engaging attendees with a challenge or a puzzle that encourages innovative thinking. These may or may not tie in directly with the focus of the meeting. The idea is to keep their creative juices flowing. The Internet is a great source for unusual trivia, or you can incorporate questions from games such as Mind Trap or Trivial Pursuit. The cards supplied with these game are ideal for periodically interjecting thought-provoking questions, and even better if you select ones that are directed toward the remainder of your meeting.

For example, if I were speaking to human resource professionals, I might challenge them with something like this: Two women, who look identical, are applying for a position in your company. They were born the same day, month, and year, and have the same mother and father. They even have the same address and phone number. You mention they obviously must be twins, but they say "No. We are honestly not twins." How is that possible? This may seem like a trick question, even though there's a very logical explanation. The answer is that they are triplets, but only two of them are present.

It can be that simple. Throwing out a curve, in particular, an unexpected question, even though it may take you off track a few moments, can go a long way in keeping your audience intact and stimulated. Your willingness to reward the right answers with an innovative mystery prize will also yield more focus.

At one conference attendees were instructed to remove their shoes and sit on the floor (which was actually plush carpeting). Pillows, notebooks, and coffee were then dispersed to create a relaxed and comfortable atmosphere for a brainstorming session. This broke down a wall that led to the most open creativity they had ever shared among themselves.

In another instance employees were requested to use cell phones to take pictures of their collaborative team efforts while completing multiple tasks during a training session. By later posting the photos for everyone else to see, it gave other teams the chance to share their advice and offer encouraging feedback. While very basic in concept, the participants found them especially invigorating due to the suggestions and questions that were spawned from the alternative points of view.

In thumbing through a *Fast Company* magazine recently, I came across an ad for an interesting hotel property in St. Louis that caught my eye. The caption read, "Meeting? We were at a meeting?" *This* is what we should be shooting for when we want people's attention. Make it a habit to collect specific ideas that capture *your* attention. It's as simple as snapping a cell phone photo to remind you of a particular moment or ripping a page out of a magazine and tossing it in a folder. Then when you browse through your collection on occasion it will stimulate your senses since these are ideas that move you emotionally.

SECTION 3:
PROACTIVE CHANGE (DEDICATION)

IT'S NOT WHAT YOU SEE—

IT'S WHAT YOU **WANT** TO SEE.

CHAPTER SEVEN

THE
INDEPENDENT
EYE

Change of Heart

'm sure you can recall a number of sports events in which everything seemed to be going perfectly for the winning team. It was as if the players were predestined to win while delivering a peak performance. Then all of a sudden, midway through the game, a new wave of confidence changed the character of the losing team. Not only would they come back to win, but also leave their admiring fans and commentators in total disbelief.

During a short break, this underdog team's coach must have said something monumentally inspiring to not only motivate each member of the team, but to help them picture the circumstances of the game with a renewed outlook. How is it possible to change their behavior and willingness to win so abruptly and so positively? How can people, whether players or supporting fans, develop such a renewed spirit when they have all but given up just moments earlier?

Now consider another scenario. If you learned that someone you trusted and knew very well was a serial killer, your image of him or her would change in a heartbeat. You would completely discredit many of the wonderful pleasantries you had previously witnessed as blatant cover-ups. That person may not have changed, but our feelings about him or her would, and they would change instantaneously.

Our perceptual world is comprised of what we accept as being true. What we consider to be truth is solely based on our beliefs. By changing what we believe, we are also simultaneously changing our real world, as we know it. Any of our former beliefs can change in a fraction of a second, as long as our new beliefs are emotionally sound.

There are endless circumstances occurring in our individual lives that are entirely out of our control. Most of us have experienced a flat tire while running late for an important commitment, or the sudden onset of bad weather when we were guaranteed a spectacular day, or the unfortunate news that someone we know has become the latest cancer victim. These events instantly change the way we feel and the way we prioritize what is important to us.

I don't think there's a more emphatic way to change our perspective than surviving a near death experience. For example, many cancer survivors find themselves on an emotional roller coaster as they trudge through and endure a long process of treatment. They've had much time to reflect and are usually the most likely to develop a renewed sense of spirit and vision in many aspects of their life.

Since I am always encouraging others to challenge themselves and push their own limits, it would be a double standard for me not to do the same for myself. When I was invited to lecture at a college in South Africa, I decided to put my own sense of fear to the test.

This part of the world is home to the largest great white sharks on the planet, many of them reaching lengths of more than twenty feet. I signed up for the chance to scuba dive with them in hopes of gaining a closer look. After descending far below the surface in the waters of False Bay, for almost two hours, I was very disappointed (and maybe equally relieved) that I wasn't able to see any. Our guide advised us that just because we didn't see them, didn't mean they didn't see us. (This gave new meaning to "seeing the invisible.") She further advised us that if we were insistent upon seeing them up close and personal, it would require feeding them... while descending among them in a shark cage.

I'm convinced that nothing ever took my breath away so quickly as that unrivaled experience. In fact, I can still see the death in their eyes as they approached me. While floating tranquilly underwater within the confines of the metal cage, large chunks of chum were being thrown off the boat to attract the sharks. When these enormous creatures instantly appeared out of nowhere, and opened their jaws in my direction, I could easily foresee myself being sliced in half with one effortless bite.

Sure, the cage theoretically protected me. The unnerving challenge, though, was that the bars were four inches apart, and I also had to deal with the buoyancy of the cage. This meant that my hands and feet would occasionally find themselves extending beyond the perimeter of its protection. It was an ever-conscious struggle hanging onto the bouncing cage within the turbulent waters, while trying to maintain all my body parts inside. Suddenly the intimidation of presenting a lecture to my respected peers at the college seemed like a much easier chore. The battles of life have a way of changing our perspective.

**Take risks not to
escape life, but
to prevent life
from escaping.**

Surviving a life threatening situation makes us keener to the finer points of our existence. Today, more than ever, the pace of life encourages a trend to skip over the minor details that may otherwise go unnoticed. However, these are time and again the most noteworthy ways to help us rise above the crowd, both in business and our personal lives. Instead of racing to compete, a more relaxed and introspective approach will usually prove more rewarding. Reflective moments are most necessary when we don't have time for them. While simple in theory, we can easily disregard this basic principle because in striving to be more efficient we have less opportunity for being open to change.

Because we are intense creatures of habit who resist the very thought of leaving our comfort zones, it can almost feel like work when we want to modify our behavior. The actual truth is we are the most adaptable species on the planet and the only one that can survive so readily, whether at the poles, the equator, or even outside our atmosphere. We can travel to the depths of our ocean waters as well as millions of miles into space. We are forever increasing our ability to adapt technology in every way possible to make life even easier. There seems to be no end to accommodating any want we have or need we can conceive.

When I reflect on our adaptability, nothing comes as close to solidifying its true meaning as an experiment we conducted with prisms while in optometry school. A prism is a clear lens with a thicker edge on one side than the other. Because of this inconsistency in the thickness, someone looking through the lens will see a shift in location of anything seen through it. The greater the difference in edge thickness the more the object will appear to shift. Prisms have been used successfully to help the eyes work better conjunctionally when one eye is predisposed to drifting inward or outward. While often referred to as being "cross-eyed," the correct name for this anomaly is strabismus.

By diffracting the incoming light into a new direction with the use of a prism, each eye is now able to focus on the same point of interest simultaneously even though they may not be physically aligned properly.

We did the experiment using our own eyes so that we would have a firsthand understanding of what a patient would experience. By placing an equal amount of prism, which was oriented in the same direction in front of both eyes, we were able to intentionally reposition our area of focus. In other words, the prism moved our focus several degrees away from where we assumed we were looking. When I attempted to pick up a pen on the desk in front of me, I would reach ten inches to the left of where it really was, over and over again.

Our intriguing revelation was that it took only a few minutes for me and the other participants to modify the way our brains had been wired since birth, and adapt to our new circumstances. We eventually learned to reach to the wrong place, purposefully, each time so we could pick up the pen with total accuracy.

When each of us removed the prisms, twenty minutes later, the exact opposite occurred. Now, using my unaltered vision, without any prisms in front of me, I began reaching ten inches to the "right" of the pen, because of my newly learned habit. Within such a short time span, my eyes had already completely adapted to the illusion that the prism created. Once again I had to retrain my thought process and associate the correct movement with the way I was seeing.

The premise that prompted my attention for participating in this fascinating experiment was another study I had learned about that was even more astounding.

What we assume we're seeing in the real world is actually projected upside down inside our eye. The image that is created on the retina is inverted. Our perception then corrects our understanding of this image which gives us a right side up perspective. In this particular study, participants wore specialized lenses that completely inverted their entire vision. Everything they saw appeared to be upside down. After a lifetime of adaptation to their vision being inverted, for the first time they saw it the way their eye actually sees it. Their whole world was reversed.

In less than two weeks the brain was able to perceive the image the way it should and automatically inverted it again. It's difficult to imagine the awkwardness of that adjustment for two whole weeks, but every person taking part in the experiment was eventually able to interpret his or her vision correctly. Then, similarly to our experiment, once the glasses were removed, it took the participants another two weeks to perceptually reverse what they saw and interpret everything as being right side up again.

A more relevant application of our vision's ability to adapt manifests itself during a contact lens fitting technique known as "monovision." Once contact lens patients reach an age where they require bifocals for close vision, a choice must be made among extra reading glasses, bifocal contact lenses, or the use of one eye for distance vision and the other one for seeing closer... known as monovision. President Reagan was one of the earlier public figures that helped to popularize this concept. While we may imagine this to be rather confusing for our vision, the brain quickly learns to place its emphasis on exactly where we choose to focus.

An illusionist, too, can take advantage of our adaptability and purposely lead our perception to a predetermined conclusion. As an example, sometimes during a performance an entertainer will incorporate a subtlety known as a "spectator's choice." Here is an example that you can weave into a group meeting when you want to emphasize a key point (or even demonstrate in a one-on-one situation, such as a sales call).

Using the assistance of someone from the group, have them step forward and circle one of three words that you have written large enough for everyone to see. As soon as they commit themselves by circling one of the words, immediately ask them if they happened to notice what is written on the marker they were handed. As they now glance down to see what you're referring to, they will be amazed to find your prediction on the marker they're still holding, which matches the very word they just selected. It's as though you knew what they were thinking before they even agreed to assist you.

While it appears as though you were intuitively able to read someone's mind, this is actually a well-orchestrated presentation that takes advantage of people's adaptability in wanting to believe something impossible. Let's say that, as in this first example above, the volunteer circles the first word. Again, your reply would be to ask them to read your prediction on the marker (which you secretly placed there beforehand).

If the person had circled the second word, instead of telling them to look at the marker, you would turn over the easel (or dry erase board, or notebook, or whatever writing surface you're using) to reveal that you were confident they would select the second word (since you had also secretly written the second word there ahead of time). And had they chosen the third word, rather than point out the pen or turn over the writing surface, you would hand them the envelope that you are still holding and had removed the marker from. In this case they would remove a small note from the envelope (that you had also placed there earlier) declaring that they would undoubtedly pick the third word. In each instance the spectators were made to feel as though this was the only form of revelation you intended to use, and their own adaptability allows them to believe that this was the solitary prediction. This is simply a variation of the business card trick explained earlier which demonstrates there are endless ways it can be presented.

We are fortunate to be so adaptive, and able to break away from the constraints of our perpetual habits. The fastest way to improve upon anything we aspire to do is to commit to seeing things from a new perspective. What old perspective can you make new?

Mind Over Matter

One morning while examining patients in my office, I had the pleasure of seeing two women in their nineties, during back-to-back appointments. When I greeted the first ninety-one-year-old lady and asked how she was doing, she finally broke her frown to retort, "Well, this will surely be the highlight of my week, so please take your time. The only thing I'll do when I get home is sit on the porch and watch my weeds grow. There just isn't a whole lot to look forward to anymore."

My very next patient was ninety-three, so just out of curiosity I asked her the same question. However, she answered quite differently, saying, "Well, I hope this won't take too long because I have gifts to buy for my daughter's birthday this weekend. And after that my church is having a social committee meeting, and I don't want to be late. Lucky for me I'll be near my favorite bookstore, too, and hopefully I'll have time to stop. So I wouldn't mind if you did this lickety split today." Not only was she inspiring, but I became so engrossed in conversation about her travels while examining her eyes, that I did lose track of time. I could have sat and listened to her captivating stories for hours.

Live every day as though it's your last and someday you'll be right.

She had so much spunk and vibrant energy, with a plethora of interests to match, that her drive to live every moment to its fullest will probably add years to her life. She actually picked my brain about my thoughts on ten-year investments! Health-wise, both patients were very mobile and on little medication for their age. Similar to the two earlier visitors from New York, the only difference between the two women was their attitude... their ability to make the optimal use of the cards they were dealt.

While at Penn State, a buddy of mine was undecided about what career path to follow. Outside of class we shared the same enthusiasm for sports and a comparable skill level in tennis, Each semester we committed to hitting the courts at least three times a week. Even though Steve had enrolled in a political science curriculum, it was obvious that his DNA had been more engineered for serving and volleying than any government policies. After months of internal searching, he finally opted to change his major to recreation and parks. He had never been excited about entering a building to go to work each day. He was hoping that his depth of knowledge in sports might lend nicely for incorporating more tennis into his life and securing his ideal job as an instructor someday.

Upon graduating, rather than looking for a high paying job to begin paying off his school loans, Steve elected to take a year off and pursue what he enjoyed more than anything else, which was playing tennis. He moved to Hilton Head Island, South Carolina and applied for an entry-level position as an assistant teaching pro at Hilton Head Plantation. Knowing that any early involvement might mean babysitting young children on the court while their parents took off to play golf, he accepted an offer and began the possibility of chasing his dream.

He wasn't there very long, though, before an opportunity arose for him to work at Palmetto Dunes, home to the Rod Laver Tennis Camp. Not only was he ecstatic to meet and work under such a tennis legend, but as each of the instructors above him left for other career choices, Steve gradually moved up the ladder until he attained a permanent position as the head teaching pro.

Living in tennis shoes, riding his bike to work each day, and hitting more tennis balls in a week than most tennis lovers hit in a year, he had woven his way into the idyllic lifestyle he had always imagined. The last time I spoke with him he could barely remember what it was like to wear long pants. Steve was dedicated and persistent, and followed a dissimilar mindset than most of his peers. By staying true to his priorities and ignoring mainstream logic, he is still living a life that many people strive for only when they retire.

Another friend of mine from high school had a similar revelation during a scuba diving vacation in St. Thomas... and, essentially, never came back. At an early age, he committed himself to pursue his passion of diving the countless reefs of the Caribbean Islands. After networking and establishing a rapport with the locals, it wasn't long before he improvised a way to make his avocation pay for itself by becoming an underwater photography expert. Today, he is still one of the most notable instructors in the area.

> **There are many more people trying to meet the right person rather than become the right person.**

Unlike the blue and green waters of St. Thomas, my early days of graduate school were especially draining. I thought Penn State was a struggle in trying to contend for the limited number of acceptances into optometry school. I had no premonition of what I was getting myself into during the next four years of working toward my doctorate. Because the college always admitted more students than they intended to keep, there was a focus on weeding out any who weren't committed to the crucial amount of work ahead.

Initially some of my classes took on an aggressive atmosphere as the professors would test our stamina for studying as well as our comprehensive retention. Many of us tackled our notes and books upwards from thirty hours a week... and that was after first attending forty hours of classes.

Academic life was a little intimidating at that point, as many of my fellow classmates were equipped with multiple degrees and even PhD's, so I knew it was going to take a desired effort to stay afloat. It was a welcomed surprise, though, when the whole class came together and agreed to deal with our workload from a refreshing point of view. Rather than increasing the competitive nature of our courses by working against each other, we chose to rally as a team in an effort to help everyone who was dedicated.

Day after day we had lectures saturated with important information. The mountains of tedious facts we were expected to retain seemed almost insurmountable. It was virtually unfeasible to take quality notes while trying to comprehend so much new material at break neck speed. As a self-made student body, we decided to elect class officers who then implemented a "note-taking service." This turned out to be a valuable safety net for trying to devour so much information. In fact, it was most likely responsible for the majority of the class ever graduating at all.

The officers probed for students in the class who had expertise and proficiencies in anatomy, physiology, biochemistry, and every other subject on our schedule. One select student was then responsible for recording all the notes in that particular class. The rest of us would just settle back and listen intently during a lecture, hoping to digest and absorb as much new material as possible. By the next day, all the notes from each class had been well organized, typed, and forwarded to each of us. A tremendous burden had suddenly been lifted from our shoulders, and we could now concentrate on learning instead of trying to take notes simultaneously.

Not every student made the cut; in fact, we lost over fifteen percent of our classmates. But it couldn't be blamed on a lack of support for each other. We accepted a motto that was continually used to encourage each other: The number one person in the class would be valedictorian. The number two person in the class would be salutatorian. And the last person in the class would be... a doctor. The focus was not on where in the class you ended up, as long as you survived to the last day. A number of students were consistently less competent at taking tests. They paradoxically proved to be some of the better clinicians in the class; we each have our strengths. (Who cares about test scores if you're not clinically proficient?)

In the same way that our note takers discovered, some of our deeply hidden talents have no reason to surface until we are challenged. The only requirement is a willingness to attempt them, and a commitment to trying something new. Imagine the vast variety of skills we may have that continually go unnoticed.

One way to make them more apparent is to start by listing some of your hobbies and compelling interests. Then create a second list of the valuable skills and knowledge you've acquired in order to enjoy or take part in each of these avocations. Now, stepping back a little, see the second list from a new vantage point. You may notice that some of these attributes might align with other mainstream occupations. For instance, if you have a hobby that requires manual dexterity and attention to detail, such as fly-fishing, then maybe it would be second nature for you to work with micro circuitry or to do laboratory analysis.

If your mind is still blank, you can further direct yourself where to look by jotting down at least seven innate attributes on the left side of a page. Now on the right side list several new skills or talents that you would like to attain. Then draw a line from each word on the left that is most closely related to (even in a very remote way) a word on the right. The words on the left will help you to jumpstart what may be an easy transition, in that learning something new on the right may require a much shorter time frame than expected. By giving in to our human nature to be curious and inquisitive, sometimes a nominal change in our perspective will open the door to something more easily attainable than we ever anticipated.

We need constant motivation since so much of our life is on auto-pilot. It's easy to keep meandering from one chore to the next without ever reminding ourselves we are constantly being educated. It's practically impossible to see the many invisible opportunities we have to learn that surround us at any given moment.

You can begin by heightening your awareness to them. Suppose, for example, that while you are driving, you want to teach yourself something new in the realm of time management. Your first instincts may be to head to a bookstore or to surf the Internet in search of new information. But there are also opportunities to learn right where you are, if you are willing to recognize them.

On a fanatical level, let's say you're currently in the process of running a handful of errands. By arranging all of your driving in a counter clockwise direction, you can now take advantage of turning right at all the red lights and save a significant amount of time. If you're also listening to an audio book while driving, you can gain knowledge about anything conceivable instead of waiting to find time to read. Keeping a reminder list at your fingertips can jog your memory about key things that still require your attention.

Some of this gets back to multi-tasking and a less efficient way to learn. Keep in mind that we arrive at some of our best ideas by a combination of being present and still allowing our thoughts to brew.

Earlier I mentioned how easily our minds are liable to drift. The more often we refocus our thinking, the greater likelihood that our mind will recognize a unique opportunity to learn. The more specific we are in how we direct our thinking, the more of a niche problem we may be able to solve.

If you were to drive by a sign that read "General Car Repairs – We Work on All Models," it would likely go unnoticed. This is basically because it blends in with the loads of similar advertisements you've seen before and there is nothing unusually distinctive about this type of business. However, if you came across a sign that promoted "Vintage

Mustang Refurbishing and Repairs – Custom and Hard to Find Parts Available," it might be more likely to catch your eye as it represents a very specific niche market. If you actually owned an early Mustang it would really funnel your attention. Even if you didn't, it could strike a chord for someone else who did, and you might be likely to tell him or her about it.

In a similar way, if someone handed me a business card that said "Quality Graphic Design," my focus might turn to questioning the true quality, knowledge, and expertise that was promised in making such a generalized statement. My immediate reaction would be "what reason do I have to choose this business over any other one?" However, if someone handed me a more specialized business card, say, "Studio 1 Graphics for the Music Industry," I might become more engrossed by such a specific niche and may even wonder who I knew that could benefit from their business, or if they might still be willing to help me. The more specified the description, the easier it becomes for us to make a choice.

In today's world we seldom make it to adulthood before reaching a saturation point. We have so many choices and not enough time. Doing something new means having to give up something else, whether it be time, money, or our attention. To get the most out of life we not only need to bring the right attitude, but also the right sense of balance. At times we want our minds to escape, still knowing the value in moving toward a finite point. The more skillfully we control our attention, the less we become distracted by so many choices.

More and more of our decision-making is challenged by invisible time constraints... the feeling that we should be doing something else. So a valuable key becomes *trusting* where we choose to focus so we can ignore what's immaterial. By doing this we not only benefit from achieving more, but by achieving what is most important to us.

While rehearsing to be in front of live audiences (and all the distractions that are imminent within such a setting) I used to practice performing illusions in front of a loud television. I trusted that if I could still maintain my train of thought with such an annoyance, any live group would be much easier.

It can be as simple as mind over matter when you endeavor to practice the skill of ignoring all of your surroundings. If you can enjoy a good book in a crowded environment, you already know how to rivet your focus while shutting out everything else.

In the Fast Lane

So why do we often feel like we're on a treadmill that's accelerating out of control? Why do our parents, and especially our grandparents, keep reminding us that life will go even faster as we age? Technology was supposed to have given us more time, but the problem is that now our concept of time is changing as our lives become ever more structured and compartmentalized.

We erroneously like to justify that the clocks of today can quantify our time the same way they did ten years ago. However, an inconsistency arises when we attempt to evaluate time externally rather than internally. We each have "one" lifetime, albeit some are longer than others, with experiences that can't be measured against a man-made timepiece. Our watch may be useful for maintaining a schedule, but not for determining the value of it.

Think back to your early years of elementary school. Didn't it seem as though the second hand barely moved, and that you waited forever for recess? When we're eight years old, each year that goes by represents an eighth of our entire life. At age forty, each year is now only a fortieth of our life. Because time is relative, so is the way we perceive our lives.

The problem is not that we have less time, but that we are forced to choose among so many opportunities.

Since each year becomes a smaller increment in the totality of our existence, it also makes each year seem shorter. From our own perspective, it is. We would like to think that the clock from our younger years is not ticking any faster. The truth is that the clock isn't, but our perspective of it surely is – for two reasons.

As young children, we had poor judgment of time because we lacked the experience of it. When I had a two-week break from school for the holidays, it was difficult to comprehend exactly how long it would take until I had to return. My vacation felt like an eternity. I just knew that one evening my mother would tell me that tomorrow I had to wake up early so I wouldn't be late for school. I had very little understanding of that frame of reference, as my world consisted of playing and fun activities with almost no time constraints.

Now we have schedules and calendars to live by, and we plan our itineraries months and even years in advance. We have a much stronger sense of how long it will take for specific dates to arrive. We know through experience how it feels for a week or a month to pass by.

The larger part of why we feel life is passing us by so swiftly, though, is that we are not *present* during a sizeable part of our day. We become ever more married to our apparent obligations. While we have the convenience of all types of electronic gadgetry, which outwardly appear to increase our efficiency, they can also make us less *effective* for how we want to live our lives. They rob us of our ability to be present in the moment. Often we find ourselves more focused on our cell phones than our children, surfing the net rather than finishing our work, and trying to meet deadlines instead of taking time to exercise and eat properly. We seldom stop to reflect whether we're making the best use of our time in a world of electronic intrusions.

Picture a family on vacation as one of the parents forever has their video camera in hand hoping to capture every moment possible for memory's sake. The person is so caught up in the little screen that he or she never becomes an integrated part of the experience itself. The person may collect a plethora of smiling faces while missing the most phenomenal aspects of the scenery and everything else that's taking place all around them. While I do enjoy photography, I realize that the pictures are primarily for me. Sure, someone may comment about the unusual scenery or interesting buildings, without ever knowing what they truly represent. When I see photographs of Petra, the Taj Mahal, or Machu Picchu, I am also reminded of the temperature that day, the smells in the air, the noise around me, the walk to get there, and what I ate afterwards... as long as I was living in the moment.

The best way to get a better grasp on the true value of time is to put it in perspective. To understand the value of a year, talk with a student who just failed a grade. To understand the value of a month, ask a mother who delivered a child four weeks premature. To understand the value of one week, discuss it with a writer who was fired for missing his deadline. To understand the value of one hour, watch an anxious patient before a first colonoscopy. To understand the value of a minute, speak to a traveler who just missed a flight. To understand the value of a second, observe the driver immediately behind a vehicle just involved in an accident. To understand the value of a millisecond, imagine all the hours of training behind a second place athlete who competed in an Olympic event.

The length of a minute depends on which side of the bathroom door you're on.

While giving a presentation in Lausanne, Switzerland, I made a discovery that has significantly changed my life ever since. I had taken advantage of visiting some local tourist destinations and, in particular, the famed university. It was there that I became especially engrossed in the studies of one of the school's professors. His name was Vilfredo Pareto. Actually born in France, he spent much of his life in Italy, where he made a remarkable observation that was reasonably consistent throughout the country.

Pareto calculated that approximately eighty percent of the property in Italy was owned by only twenty percent of its residents. His theory was based on an earlier study by Joseph Juran who discovered that this principle actually holds true for many aspects of society. This law of 80/20, also commonly referred to as the law of the vital few, is often regarded as the Pareto Principle. As an interesting sidebar, since Juran is the one who first conceptualized its usefulness, many authorities give him more of the credit and are even hoping to rename the principle in his honor.

Essentially it contends that eighty percent of all success comes from a specific twenty percent of the effort that's put into it. Therefore, this would imply that eighty percent of our productivity comes from a mere twenty percent of what we do. Twenty percent of a company's workforce is likely responsible for eighty percent of the company's revenue. Equally true is that eighty percent of car accidents are perhaps caused by twenty percent of the drivers. And twenty percent of your purchases are probably responsible for eighty percent of your garbage. This basic concept was found to touch almost every facet of our lives.

It would follow that the ideal scenario for us, then, is to find and focus on this valuable twenty percent of what we do to reap the maximum rewards. Let's assume that we have written five items on a list of what we hope to accomplish today. Invariably we tend to do the easiest ones first, because it makes us feel productive when we're able to cross a couple of these off our list. Heck, if we can even cross three things off we can pat ourselves on the back for completing more than half of the work... right? Well, the problem is that we usually dwell on the eighty percent that's often much quicker and easier to deal with, because this still offers us a sense of accomplishment. What we don't comprehend is how much we are deceiving ourselves, based on the Pareto Principle.

Because of this "law of the vital few," which appears quite valid according to my own investigation, one of those five things would seem to be four times more important to do than anything else on our list. But let's examine this a little closer. What it's actually saying is that if one item is worth eighty percent of our success, and the other four are only worth twenty percent *combined*, then each of those four is only contributing five percent to our accomplishments.

If one of those items is worth eighty percent of our success compared to the others being only five percent, that means that the first one is *sixteen* times more important than each of the others. We hastily look at the items on our list that are the easiest to do because it provides us with a quick, but false, sense of accomplishment. This principle demonstrates that you will be sixteen times more effective to work on the one most important thing, even if you don't finish it, than to piddle away at any of the less significant ones.

The speed of time is one second per second. Our success is determined by how we use it.

Any time not spent working on the most valuable item on your list is not only a poor use of your time, it's actually taking you away from your ultimate goals at a much faster rate than you imagine.

There was a time in the past when we, as a work force, had to physically make the things we needed. Now we have automated machinery to make most of what we require. So instead of making things, we make decisions.

Most of our lives are based on decision-making. Working longer hours doesn't necessarily make us more productive, because it doesn't guarantee that we will also make better decisions. In fact, quite often the contrary is even true. Some people have the knowledge and experience to make superior decisions in a very short period of time. Obviously, that can be much more lucrative than working overtime and making inferior decisions.

Contrary to what we believe, we can make quality decisions but we cannot plan quality time. We may attempt to allocate quality time, say an hour of non-interruption with our child on a Saturday afternoon, but that doesn't necessarily mean it will be quality time. What we need to do is spend *enough* time, and the results will be occasional moments of quality time. When playing golf, we can plan to make our next hole the best one of the day, but that won't necessarily happen. It may motivate us or encourage us, but it's not until we swing at enough balls that we eventually play some noteworthy holes.

It's quite incredible that in today's world there are still a few primitive cultures in remote parts of Africa and South America that don't rely on time at all. There are no clocks or watches to be found anywhere, and not having any source of a time element means that they continuously live in the present. While our never ending lists of commitments place us on a tightly wired schedule, the less we glance at our timepieces, the more we take ownership of being in "the now."

Too often we get caught up in the frenzy of keeping up with society. We may start to feel partially inadequate and yearn for a new temporary sense of accomplishment (which is only exacerbated by our electronic ability to see how everyone else is getting ahead of us). Our existence can become a blur... much like certain aspects of the picture on the next page.

You'll notice that there appear to be gray spots at the intersections of the white lines. But when we look directly at any specific crossing, the gray spots disappear. Our eyes continue to chase these ghostly gray areas in an endless state of quandary, similar to the impatient way that we sometimes conduct our lives.

I remember witnessing an employee in a corporate lunchroom standing next to a microwave. She punched in thirty seconds and almost immediately began snapping her fingers saying, "Come on. Come on. I don't have all day."

Is this what our world has come to? Are we so impatient that we can't even relax for thirty seconds? It seems the faster technology is able to serve us, the more impatient we become. Racing against time, or to a higher standard of living, doesn't always equate to a higher "quality" of life. Working harder, faster, and longer is not the answer to making more prudent decisions. There is a common saying that I learned in Scotland that states: "If you want to have a baby it will take nine months. You can't put nine women on it and expect them to finish in one month."

As hard as we may try, it is impossible to remember any complete individual days. But what we can remember are numerous significant moments... which means that living in the present is the most valuable input we have in making our lives more meaningful.

Life is not measured by the number of breaths we take, but by the number of moments that take our breath away.

Wouldn't you like to double your life expectancy? Understanding the concepts above will allow us to do just that. If we practice living in the present and collect twice as many moments we cherish, isn't that essentially the same as living two lifetimes that have only half the significance? I am reminded again of my two ninety-year-old patients to live each day to the fullest.

When people complain about how inundated they feel from their heavy workloads, sometimes I offer the following analogy as a little comic relief. It references quality time versus overtime and why they should never feel as though they're being treated unfairly.

There are three hundred and sixty-five days in the year. Most everyone in the United States is allowed two weeks off for vacation. So if we take those fourteen days away that leaves us with three hundred and fifty-one.

Most people also work a traditional eight-hour day, which means that the other sixteen hours, or two thirds of the day, is free. So if we remove two-thirds of that time, it leaves one hundred and seventeen workdays. The majority of people don't work Saturdays or Sundays either, and there are fifty-two of each of those every year. So if we knock those one hundred and four days out of the picture, that actually leaves us thirteen days.

And since there are six national holidays each year, New Year's Day, Memorial Day, Fourth of July, Labor Day, Thanksgiving, and Christmas, we'll remove those six, too. So now that leaves us with only seven days, or essentially, one workweek. No one should ever complain when they really only work one week a year. (The only reason why this might sound plausible to someone is that there are three types of people... those who can count, and those who can't.)

For the next three hours, try hard not to let the clock dictate any of your thoughts. When taking a vacation, rather than trying to "do Europe in a week," immerse yourself in an area of one country (even where you are now) and savor it for all it's worth... it will be much more enriching. Using the finite time you have available, practice disregarding things of lesser value and try focusing on fewer things that are more significant to you.

False Frame

It's been said that "a task will often take the time allotted." This probably rings true because we tend to over estimate how difficult a task might actually be. We may assume that it takes monumental changes to improve some of our capabilities. But it's easy to overlook the simplest methods for self-improvement.

We are much more motivated by pain than pleasure. When an auto mechanic recommends that we update a worn out part of our engine, there is little pleasure in spending money for the peace of mind we'll soon forget. If our car breaks down, we are suddenly very willing to pay the price in exchange for the discomfort of not having a dependable vehicle. Pain is a much stronger instigator.

In another instance, suppose a charitable organization is conducting a fund drive and is seeking large donations for their cause. If the only promotional effort consists of volunteers touting empty cans at a busy intersection, we may not be willing to be very generous. But if we were invited to an event displaying heart wrenching photographs of victims unsettled by tragedies, which gradually tugged on our emotions, this would undoubtedly create a stronger form of leverage.

A previously mentioned friend of mine is regularly searching for people that will potentially invest large sums of money to back new entertainment acts for television and major resorts. He frequently has the chore of approaching complete strangers and asking them for millions of dollars, and often he succeeds. To do this, he must help them to envision a very appealing outcome. His challenge is to sell the probability of an unknown act to someone who appreciates this type of risk and has the ample capital necessary.

When he offers someone the perfect chemistry of excitement, potential earnings, and pride of ownership, an agreement can sometimes be reached rather swiftly. Without his ability to visualize an end result, a project of this scale would never gain any traction.

You can do the impossible if you can visualize the invisible.

Sure, with maturity and experience we consistently learn to make better and faster decisions. But in today's world of self-reliance, and using the Internet as our primary source for information, we shouldn't overlook another valuable resource that's too easy to take for granted. Because of our ability to share so much information electronically, our society has begun to lose the art of conversation. Don't underestimate the value of every interaction you have with other people, whether they are trusted experts, good friends, or absolute strangers. When you are present and enjoying the moment with an open mind you will learn much by observing, and even more by sharing time with the most diverse people possible.

There is something rather unique and more revealing about having a live conversation with someone who can express their thoughts, opinions, and other points of reference in a way that can't be duplicated in a text message or an email. Facial contours and verbal inflections can convey much more than the words themselves.

Sometimes the primary justification for seeking outside help with our decision-making is to help keep our wandering focus on track. Most professionals will agree that working with a coach will not only help you to stay on target but ensure that you reach your goals much faster. It's so easy to become distracted that we don't perceive when it's happening. Because this is such an effective component for success, there are numerous organizations of retired business professionals and senior corporate advisors who donate their time to helping others make better informed choices, both in business and in balancing their personal life.

It's hard to create balance in what we do if we neglect it in what we see. Imagine that you are building a house and the contractor wants to discuss the entranceway for your new dwelling. What component of the doorway is most important? What aspect of it deserves the most attention? Is it in finding an unusual doorknocker or the safety that a security bolt would provide? Or is it the hinges, or possibly the door handle, since the door would not be functional without either of them?

The Zen philosophy to this question is that the door itself is the least important aspect compared to the space or opening that allows you to pass through. While the decorative hardware of the door itself may be dramatic and steal our attention, it's the size and depth of the opening that are most critical and significant for its function. It's easy to become distracted by bright and shiny objects.

Our most basic and fundamental level of thinking focuses on things. A higher level of understanding focuses on people. And our highest level of intelligence focuses on ideas. There are a variety of objects and people constantly transitioning through our field of view and, therefore, commanding the majority of our attention. But they are also the primary reason why so many great ideas are invisible to us, because our "things" get in the way.

As our society becomes more affluent, we are inclined to put far too much focus on the "objects" in our lives, hoping to satisfy a thirst that is inexhaustible. As referenced previously, we find ourselves saying,

"If I just had a faster computer I'd be happy." And after that it's, "If I only had more closet space, I wouldn't ask for anything else." And then, "If I simply had a boat, I'd be content forever." But these objects, regardless of their size or expense, have a very short shelf life of happiness as we will never feel completely satisfied when it comes to physical things.

You may argue that you're already exceedingly content with all the toys you own, but this concept stretches into other areas of our lives that we take for granted, too.

If we look at a standard home of just fifty years ago, they all had very small bathrooms. They were functional for what we needed and nothing more. The newer homes built twenty-five years later not only had larger bathrooms that you could walk around in, but many had separate oversized tubs that almost resembled a spa. Now, we are building bathrooms larger than our former living rooms. Some of them are complete with huge closets and dressing areas, and we have companies whose sole business is custom furnishings and refinishing for bathrooms. *Rightsizing Your Life* by Ciji Ware is an interesting read about how to simplify our surroundings while keeping what matters most. Do we really need two potato peelers, three vacuum cleaners, and four televisions?

The ability to enjoy physical luxuries only provides a temporary form of contentment, as we look to our family, friends, and relationships for a more meaningful form of fulfillment. But, again, it's too easy to lose our focus among all the propaganda and marketing in today's society. As a young student I was given an interesting book titled *Hope for the Flowers* by Trina Paulus, which appeared to be written for children, but the message within its pages is certainly beneficial for any adult. It brings to light how our competitive nature so easily gets the best of us. We inadvertently lose sight of the true spirit of life in our never-ending quest to reach the top, whatever that may be.

You can purchase an employee by virtue of a high salary, but you can't buy a caring and trusting friend. One of the finest sources for our growth and development is the people that we choose to envelop ourselves with. Take a moment to write down the winning quarterback of the 1993 Super Bowl, two recipients of the 2000 Nobel Peace Prize, and three actors who won 2007 Oscar awards. These are legendary people who have received a massive amount of press and television exposure, and may have even had an impact on our lives. At one time these six people were front-page news and possibly household words, yet now we are hard pressed to remember them.

Now make a second list of three trusted friends, two former teachers, and a relative that has significantly influenced your life. It could be a person you seldom speak with, someone who's no longer living, or anyone that you feel influenced you in a constructive way. Remember that these are the people who are much more valuable in shaping our personal lives than the hundreds of people we temporarily choose to sensationalize.

A significant life impacts the lives of others.

There's a commonly told story of a schoolteacher who was giving an important exam to his class, but the students were a little confused by his last question. The question asked for the name of the school's custodian. As one student finished and handed her test to the instructor, she asked if this was some sort of a joke. The teacher replied by saying this was indeed as important as any other question, and it would be counted equally. He went on to explain this custodian plays an integral part in the cleanliness of the entire school, which affects the students' lives each day. In life, we will meet many people who will have a positive impact on us, and it's important to remember their names, too.

One day, about ten years after graduating from optometry school, I thought back to all the people that helped me along the way with my education. From the lesson about the custodian above, I decided to write several thank-you notes to the teachers who had a major influence on me.

One of them was my physical education instructor, Pete Leach. On the first day of class, he was reminiscent of a stereotypical drill sergeant, often shouting at the top of his lungs, and we were all deathly afraid of him. He came down hard on anyone who appeared to be giving only ninety percent of their effort. I later learned that inside that tough outer skin, though, was a truly caring heart that wanted everyone to excel. He taught me much more about dedication and perseverance than I could ever learn from a textbook. In his gruff and still somewhat barking voice, he immediately called me after receiving my note to say how much he appreciated the words I shared with him after all these years.

A few years later, at the early age of fifty-nine, Pete died unexpectedly from a heart attack. Attending his funeral service out of respect for a family I had never met was without question. Upon arriving that day, I wasn't shocked to see one of the largest crowds I had ever witnessed for a viewing. It seems I was not the only one who had appreciated the depth of his character.

I finally reached the family to share my condolences. I mentioned my name and that I was one of his former students. "Oh my gosh, 'you're' the one!" his wife and daughter exclaimed. At first I felt terrible, worried that I may have offended them in some way, but then they pulled me aside to say, "You're the person who wrote the letter! Do you realize that he kept it in the top drawer of his dresser and looked at it weekly for the remainder of his life? He would always comment, 'This is why I became a teacher, and this is what's really important to me.' We put your letter in the casket, as we know he would want it with him. Thank you for reminding him he made a difference."

In all probability, for the first time in my life I understood how significant a few simple words can be and how dramatically they can affect someone's spirit. I went home that night with the realization that even the smallest of efforts can have a meaningful and lasting effect. It only made me wish I had written more notes and not to wait before writing more. (The above story taught me why texting and emails don't carry a fraction of the weight as a hand written note or a live conversation.) Inevitably people are more influenced by how much we care than how much we know.

It's one thing to hear an older person claim how rapidly time erodes based on our earlier arguments. It's a real wake up call when the first and second graders I examine insist that time seems to be going faster for them, too. Life is much too short to keep our thumb on the fast forward button. As a society, we are quick to focus on people's flaws rather than what's below the surface. Occasionally we need to hit the pause mode and take a moment to appreciate some of the people we take for granted.

Having lived just outside of Hollywood, I was aware of a young actress who was always being ridiculed about the size of her nose. Her peers increasingly encouraged her to undergo cosmetic surgery if she wanted to stay on the radar in such a competitive industry. Though her career seemed to be on a continual climb, she decided to have the surgery anyway. How ironic that ever since her nose was modified she never found a major role again. Often the very thing we like to criticize is what gives us our character and makes us unique.

> **Two things that we can never get back are the time that has already passed and the words we have already spoken.**

It's easy to become too judgmental when not taking time to form our own opinions. When we fall victim to the patterns that society creates, we miss opportunities that are there for the taking. Instead of jumping into classes on how to keep up, we may benefit more by studying ways we can slow ourselves down. At the end of each day, take a moment to reevaluate whether or not your pace was appropriate for what you really needed to accomplish. Could you have savored certain parts of the day more? How?

True Frame

There's an often-told story about two shoe salesmen that were sent to Africa in search of new markets for their company. The first salesman calls back to advise, "No one here even wears shoes, so they have no use for any of our products. This place would be a complete waste of our time." The second salesman then calls back to announce, "No one wears shoes here, so this could be a new and exciting market for us. If we act quickly we can build strong relationships with our new consumers and monopolize the whole region. How soon can we get started?"

When we truly want to see things from an isolated perspective, as well as slow down and detox from our normal routine, it can be helpful to immerse ourselves in a completely foreign environment. For that reason, my friend Rob and I signed up for an expedition into the Amazonian jungles of Peru. It was the antithesis and perfect remedy for ten lane highways, too many fast food chains, and nine hundred channels. We would have no connection with civilization as we know it and be at least a day's travel from any modern conveniences.

With the help of a local guide, whom we immediately became dependent on for both food and our safety, we soon learned what the term "survival" really meant. Despite that we were in a rainforest, our first and biggest challenge was hydration and we learned to drink from plants. The water from some roots was poisonous, while others were safe. It was a long study through a nonstop variety of vegetation before we could begin to tell the difference.

In my wildest dreams I never would have guessed we would develop a dependency on termites, but as soon as our insect repellents ran out, they became a welcomed sight. Whenever we found large termite nests in the trees, we actually moaned a sigh of relief. Our guide would use his machete to slice open the huge nest. Then we would place our hands right into the middle of it allowing the termites to crawl all over them. Within fifteen seconds our hands would be covered in black with these oversized (much larger than any I've seen in the States) wood-eaters. We would then remove our hands and smash and crumble their bodies onto our faces and necks as a form of nature's freely available insect repellent. The good news is that it really worked. Astoundingly, because these insects were busy consuming wood most of the day, they actually smelled like many of the insect repellents anyone could purchase commercially.

When we stumbled upon some of the river natives, indigenous to the area, we came face to face with some of the most primitive lifestyles on the face of the planet. I come from an area near Amish settlements in eastern Pennsylvania. Without the conveniences of electricity and modern transportation, the Amish still live a very luxurious life compared to these inhabitants. We were always welcomed into any of their crudely built huts, and they immediately shared anything they owned no matter how hard and long they had to work for it.

Some possessions are worth very little until they are given away.

It was as if they respected an invisible law of not having true possessions. They felt that everything they had came from the earth and were openly willing to give it right back to anyone else on earth, too. In any of their homes, it was safe to assume that if you wanted something it was yours, since it was equally shared by everyone.

However, outside their refuge we could not assume our safety. Unlike the African plains filled with large cats and wildebeests, these jungles were teaming with the tiniest of creatures, which were even more deadly. Our lives were literally in the hands of our native guide, who was as comfortable in these surroundings as we are with our Blackberries. What a surreal adventure and educational experience for opening our minds and seeing the world from a much removed perspective.

We definitely create more impact on our thoughts when we make physical changes around us. We don't have to go very far from home if we have the right emotional and intellectual mindset.

Not long after I returned, our church agreed to help sponsor five young refugee boys from Sudan who had migrated the whole way to Kenya on foot. Their families, mostly from the Dinka and Nuer tribes, had been murdered during civil uprisings, and they had become part of the seventeen thousand orphans found wandering for almost a decade. While many succumbed to the harsh conditions of Africa, others resorted to drinking their own urine for hydration and at times eating mud in the anguish of hoping to make their stomachs feel full.

After arriving in the U.S., the first time they encountered a stairway the boys stooped down on their hands and knees to negotiate it like any other hill... they had never seen someone use steps before in their lives. During their first trip to a grocery store, where they were inundated with the amount of food and choices, they became very confused about the isle of pet food. "Do you mean all this food here is for animals?" they questioned. "We would have been glad to eat any of this when we were on our own."

It's one thing to read this on a page of a book. It's another to look into the eyes of a child telling this story and actually feel his emotions. We need to train our eyes to see more than just what's on the surface. I recently learned of a science teacher who wanted to remind his class to be cautious about what their eyes had chosen to see. He displayed a large jar filled to the brim with rocks. He queried the students about whether or not the jar was full. Could he fill it anymore without breaking the glass, he asked, and they all agreed that he couldn't.

Then he reached under his table and grabbed a container of tiny pebbles. He poured the pebbles over the rocks as they squeezed into every little space within the jar, completely filling it. The students felt a little naïve as he asked them if they now agreed that the jar was full. The tiny pebbles seemed to occupy every little area possible, and they agreed that it was completely full. Next he reached down and brought up another container filled with sand. He poured the sand all over the pebbles and the tiny granules made their way into the very tiniest of cracks to make the jar even fuller than it was before. At this point, everyone felt rather foolish as they realized they had been making very limiting assumptions about his playful demonstration.

He wondered if the students would finally agree that the jar was now full, and very reluctantly, they nodded. He had gotten them two times in a row, but obviously nothing else could possibly fit in there now. But he removed one last container; this one filled with water. Pouring it over the rocks and sand, he was able to empty its contents into any remaining void that was previously occupied by air. He made a lasting impression in that there's always room for improvement and ways to make things more complete, even when we feel we are already finished. The difference is in where we direct our focus.

Now that we have exhausted all possibilities, let's get started.

In most civilized areas of the world, we are fortunate to have good healthcare and many resources for optimal vision, except that much more of our success and achievements come from where we choose to look as opposed to how clearly we actually see.

Imagine that you and a friend are hiking up a mountain. You decide to turn your scenic climb into a challenge to see which of you can reach the highest point first. You are allowed to choose any trail you like or even create your own path to reach the uppermost elevation. Intent on winning, you shrewdly place all your focus keenly on the trail in front of you. Not wanting to waste a precious second by enjoying the adjacent scenery or tripping on an irregular surface, your gaze is directly in front of you and fixed on the trail you've chosen. Because of this you immediately gain a quick lead on your friend who is more casually enjoying the view. His attitude seems to be much less intense as he stops on occasion to reflect on everything he sees.

All of a sudden your friend notices a higher peak than the one both of you are on. Because of the contour of the mountain, it was not visible from the bottom. Although he must first descend to reach it, before he can start climbing again, the new trail turns out to be much less demanding and even more direct. Since there are far fewer objects to navigate around it also proves to be much faster. He started out at a slower pace than you, but he managed to reach a higher peak more quickly by virtue of where he chose to look. While both of you shared the same vantage point at the start, your friend was able to win by simply taking time to notice what advantages were available to him. (This is very similar to Kodak, ignoring its competition.)

It's easy to forget the possibility of seeing things from an infinite number of angles and a variety of levels. So many aspects of what we do deserve a fresh perspective. All too often we get complacent and tolerate an incredibly narrow window.

While attending Penn State I was consciously aware of how critical a high grade point average would be for acceptance into a graduate program such as optometry school. Like most freshmen, I was required to take a general education English class but mine was taught by a new and rather incompetent teaching assistant. After ten weeks of having us write very subjective essays, he gave everyone a B for the course with very little explanation. All of my classmates were accepting of the outcome, but I couldn't afford to let this entry level course tarnish my career. I met with him, along with the head of the department, to challenge my grade for the class.

Probably because I built a respectable case for my writing, and also because the instructor was new, the department head was agreeable to changing my grade to an A. One single grade may seem insignificant during the course of my education; however, it gave me the courage to challenge another grade that was also a "judgment call." Later the combined relevance of both of those grades became instrumental for my acceptance into several graduate schools.

Near the end of optometry school I put this lesson to practice. I was in desperate need of a more dependable means of transportation beyond my high-mileage car that had barely endured all my trips to Philadelphia. I approached a number of car dealerships, and each salesperson would end our conversation by giving me a business card with his or her hand-written price on the back. I was fascinated by the wide range of quotes based on what they guessed my vehicle might be worth as a trade.

Realizing, once more, that this was a very subjective number, I used a blank business card from one of the dealerships and decided to create my own number. The next time I approached a salesperson and showed him the number I hoped he could beat for my business, he worked much harder at crunching his numbers, and I received a better deal than I thought was possible. I am certain that the dealership still came out ahead, or he wouldn't have sold me the car, but at least I was able to quickly put things into perspective of what I was willing to spend.

A few years later, using this same lesson again, I found it helpful in purchasing my first home. While banks and mortgage lenders publish a daily list of interest rates that seem to be set in stone, I found them to be equally negotiable, by starting with a competitor's offer. The same philosophy also became helpful with my mortgage.

> **If you have a problem that can be solved with money, it's not a problem, it's an expense.**

There are times when the introduction of a new reference point can aid in the consideration of another perspective. Instigating a change in someone else's perception can be equally as helpful as changing our own.

Illusionists must take advantage of unique perspectives when problem solving and trying to create new performance pieces. They are continually searching for enthralling concepts that not only captivate people visually, but intellectually and emotionally as well. His or her ultimate goal is to suspend someone's disbelief. Most of them will never hesitate to accept the challenge of inventing something new for television or a large event without having any idea how they are going to accomplish it... at least not initially.

I have several magician friends who were given the green light to perform on prime time network television, but they were expected to create something spectacular... such as levitating a car or vanishing a dozen people all at once. They would say, "Sure, no problem," and it was only then that the brainstorming began. This is a classic example of reverse thinking in that they had to visualize what they had already accomplished, and then back track to work out a possible solution. There was never any doubt of whether or not it could be done. It was just a matter of finding the most practical and cost-effective way to orchestrate the eventual performance.

The goal of an illusionist is to sharpen the sense of wonder in others.

As mentioned earlier, we lose our ability to focus on closer objects with age due to a phenomenon known as Presbyopia. But someone who is usually remembered for many other things, Benjamin Franklin, used reversed thinking in order to solve his own problem with seeing better at close range.

Knowing that the focal point of a lens couldn't be altered, he invented the first "bifocal" lens which was much more convenient for him. It enabled him to see at several distances simultaneously. While the quality of transitioning between the various focal points has technologically improved (most people now use a multi-focal lens known as a progressive), the general concept he developed has remained the same for hundreds of years.

There are certain instances, though, in which I have to solve a patient's problem with customized bifocal lenses that are unique for that individual. I have one patient who competes in target shooting and requires a customized bifocal on just one lens to assist him in lining up the sights on his firearm. These glasses would be a nuisance in most other aspects of his life. But for this specific avocation, especially in competition, they are absolutely ideal.

Imagine the situation of another patient who's an artist and wants to look off to the right at a landscape and then back to her canvas to paint what she sees. I had to create a vertical bifocal for her instead of the customary horizontal pattern. The left sides of both lenses were made to focus up close since that is the side where she would place her easel. The right sides of both lenses, where she would look to see her subject, were made to help her see better in the distance. Obviously they are only helpful to her when she wants to paint, but they are the perfect solution for her particular needs.

I have many patients that are house painters, electricians, vehicle mechanics, etc., who all do work above their heads for extended periods of time. It's become more and more common to supply them with dual bifocals, one on the top of each lens and another on the bottom. Each added lens area is customized for the distances they need most. Most often anyone's specific needs can be accommodated by simply not accepting a traditional way of thinking.

It's easy to restrict our focus to the available choices, rather than creating something entirely new and exactly what we want. If money were not a contingency, what new product would you invent that could free up ten percent of your work day? The most challenging part of the answer is in first ignoring everything else that you already know.

Premium Insurance

A professor from Harvard University made a fascinating discovery during the course of a fifty-year study. Dr. Ed Banfield was amazed to learn that the most critical factor necessary for individuals wanting to improve their financial platform and social status was long-term perspective. Few of us have *committed* long-term goals, as we are likely to focus on what is much more attainable in the short term. Unfortunately, there are many people who live day to day with no goals at all.

I remember an instance when my friends and I were shooting hoops in college. It was late at night, and we were at an indoor gym that was about to close at midnight. We continued to ignore reminders from the custodian as we were having too much fun. Then suddenly the lights went out. It was pitch black. I spun around and all I could see was the slight glow of a red exit sign. By the time I turned back again, I had lost all my orientation within the room, but I did manage to retain an interesting thought.

I had a ball in my hand, and I knew that the concept was to throw it through the hoop. But I could have spent all of eternity trying to do that without any light, because I no longer had a target or goal... at least not one that was visible. I could have thrown balls in all directions and at many distances forever in the dark without any success.

Now if someone planted me at the foul line in the direction of the backboard, in time I might have been lucky enough to sink a basket. Having a feel from previous experience and using the noise of missed shots off the rim and backboard to guide me, eventually it's conceivable that I could score even in the dark. This has acted as a metaphor for much of my life in that a goal can only be reached if it's plainly visible. The more we point ourselves in the right direction, the less time we will spend throwing away wasted shots in the dark.

In sports, business, and personal life, you will miss a hundred percent of the shots you never take.

Many of us have been encouraged at one time or another to imagine ourselves being much older than the present. We are asked to think backwards about our regrets, knowing that we still have the chance to make a difference. The problem with this excellent visualization exercise is first, most of us have heard it so often it's all too familiar and almost redundant. Second, while it sounds good in theory, most of us don't know how to get our arms around the concept to make it feel real.

One way to tackle this problem is to mentally and *physically* alter the way we feel. What may initially seem like a ridiculous waste of time may actually be the leverage required to help you fully understand. Begin by putting on some dark sunglasses and earpieces from your audio headset (or any type of ear plugs) but without any audio device attached. Next sit on a couple of tennis balls to purposely make your seat uncomfortable as you make your breathing more labored and inconsistent. This is not to say that all older people feel this way, but professional actors use this same technique to help them develop a better feel for a particular character role.

Now visualize yourself with more wrinkled skin and a back that won't straighten despite all your efforts. These physical changes in how you see and feel should assist your mindset in constructing a more believable image of yourself as you age. Finally, imagine a great loss of energy and that the days of doing anything but keeping up with your medications and doctor's visits are long gone. Take a few moments to really be inside this person you've just created, which could someday really be you. Now that you've arrived here, imagine if it were somehow possible to magically go back in time. What would you do differently before reaching this stage of your life?

This will seem far too childish for some, and the ten minutes required to gather these few props will require too much effort for others, but the rewards are unpredictably enlightening and could even change the course of your life. By changing the way you feel physically, it's much easier to keep your mind relevant with the emotional state that you're trying to create. Sometimes we have to compel ourselves into finding new ways to think.

One of the most important strategies for developing new ideas was acknowledged by two-time Nobel Prize winner Linus Pauling. His contention was that one idea alone is not enough. The ability to take an idea from concept to completion is totally a percentage game. Some ideas will work and others won't. So obviously the more ideas we have the greater our chances that one or more of them will be successful.

This means that we should try to rack up as many failures as possible because the probability of our success will go up proportionately. The most likely winner will be the one who has failed most often... first.

In the same way, a professional photographer will never take just one picture of an important subject. If he takes a hundred pictures there's a much greater chance that one will end up on the front of National Geographic or an album cover. From the standpoint of Pauling's study it will take, on average, a minimum of fifty good ideas to generate one superb idea.

Envision yourself as one of five hundred photographers, all seeking recognition. If all of you were asked to photograph an apple, how could you make one of your pictures stand out from everyone else's? There are only so many sides to an apple, and even then, they might all have a tendency to look the same. So how can you stretch your imagination to create a picture amazingly unlike all the rest? The way to solve the problem is not to look for one outstanding picture, but to imagine an infinite number of ways it could be photographed.

> **If you know what a painting's supposed to be before you paint it, then there's no reason to paint it.** —Salvador Dali

Could you change the lighting, not only in terms of brightness but also with shadows, both on and around the apple? Could the shadows have distinct shapes that would bring another element into the composition? Could you use colored lighting to dramatize and enhance the setting? Could you shoot it from underneath a glass tabletop, or through colored glass, or the reflection of a mirror? Could you shoot it after aging it from heat, after slicing it into an infinite number of configurations, or after it's been dropped from a high building? Are there interesting textures or other objects that can be placed on or around the apple to create a different mood? Has it been partially eaten by a person, or an animal, or is it still hanging from a tree?

Once we realize that there are an infinite number of ways to look at the same object, coming up with just fifty becomes an easier assignment. Just one of those might qualify as a stunning success.

CHAPTER EIGHT

UNTHINKING INSIDE THE BOX

Room with a View

One key way to help motivate ourselves as mentioned earlier is to continually change our environment. How often do you recline in the exact same place when you want to relax? Did you ever notice that most people will sit in the same seat for lunch, or the same pew in church, week after week? Even at home, firing new neurons can be as simple as sitting in a seldom-used chair, which forces us to change our perspective of the room and even modify our posture. It may also help to reposition the chair so that it doesn't face the center of the room, but instead a window or just a corner. Many readers will glance over this idea and discount it as being far too trivial, but sometimes a concept this simple will provide the necessary trigger we require for a new perspective.

Once while consulting with a large company, I suggested that one of the top executives (who had a spectacular view of the city from his private corner office) exchange work areas for one day with a support staff person who shared a module with six other employees. It was easy to implement (since each person had their own laptop), cost them nothing for the experiment, and the results were rather eye opening.

After the initial adjustment period and grumbling about her lack of privacy, the executive began to notice certain efficiencies she hadn't tried that others in the room were using to their advantage. She, in turn, was able to point out specific ways that they could improve their phone skills based on her own experiences.

The employee, who for the first time felt empowered by the surroundings of an executive suite, began developing a confidence he had never experienced before. Posting one of the better inside sales days he ever had, much of the lesson he experienced stayed with him.

Another stimulus for activating the far corners of our brain is to read something that we would characteristically not find interesting. If you are used to reading fiction, try reading more non-fiction. Or, if you normally read about travel, take a stab at reading about landscaping, origami, or a biography.

Stepping in another direction, you might be pleasantly surprised at what happens when you subtly change what you smell. Our olfactory nerves create some of the strongest associations we own. A few dollars spent on a scented candle or a scent plug for your room may also help you discover an unexplored territory in your head..

Stimulating any of our senses can nurture unanticipated results for innovative thinking. It can be invigorating to experiment at an ethnic restaurant and allow our taste buds to notice something new. It's also helpful to be intentionally open to unfamiliar types of music and unusual audio books. Your visual senses are even easier to explore by watching non-mainstream movies. One movie that stands out to me for teaching nonconformity is *Dead Poet's Society* starring Robin Williams (released in 1989). As an instructor at an all-boys preparatory school, Williams' character teaches his students the importance of seeing the world with a new set of eyes.

One of his examples for creating a novel perspective was to simply have his students stand on a desk. Even most business professionals are well aware that when they are speaking on the phone they are much more focused and intent if they are standing rather than sitting. If their conversations involve real problem solving you'll also find them pacing. This is usually not out of nervousness but to help channel more energy into their point of focus.

Other movies, like *What the Bleep Do We Know?* and *Expelled* are also very thought provoking. They each remind us that we haven't begun to scratch the surface of the pool of information that has yet to be revealed. We need constant stimulation if we want to see beyond our daily rituals and open our sense of wonder.

If it's too much of an inconvenience to turn this page upside down to read, then you're not ready to begin exploring your world in a way that's inconsistent with what has already been done over and over again for centuries. If you're really ready to take a step in a direction that will force you to see things from a challenging perspective, try holding the next page upside down, even though it's printed correctly, and see how quickly you can read it. Then place the following page in front of a mirror to determine whether or not you still have the skills to decipher it. If you can master both of these, try turning this book right side up and placing this paragraph in front of a mirror and see if you can remember what you've already read here.

Worth the Risk

Since I like to encourage others to learn through experience, I'm always looking for interesting and unorthodox ways to challenge myself and ignite my own imagination. One of the more frightening moments of my life was the decision to jump out of a plane at 12,500 feet. It could have been much more terrifying had I not done any preparation. Taking an in-depth class on how to sky-dive afforded me some peace of mind, but in all honesty, an equally anxiety-ridden moment was in signing a waiver listing all the possible things that could go wrong. I counted thirty-three times I was required to initial the various releases and indemnity clauses. I can still remember, very precisely, how the last one read: "Shit happens, no guarantees."

Many of us don't fully appreciate the difference between a chance and a risk, which are nowhere near the same. Had I jumped out of the plane without a parachute, I would clearly have had very little chance of survival. By wearing the correct safety equipment, learning about the proper way to use it, having a professional diver close at hand, and familiarizing myself with what I could expect during my first jump, it became a very low risk.

I had to visualize and practice how to keep myself from spinning, exactly when to release and open my shoot, and how to guide myself toward the target landing area. As I became more familiar with each of these steps, it kept pushing me into a lower risk category.

The basic formula for success consists of maximizing our opportunities while minimizing our risks. If we're not challenging ourselves on a regular basis, we diminish the chances we have to excel. There are many people from other countries that have a better comprehension of this than we do.

It may surprise you to learn that immigrants who arrive in the United States are *four* times more likely to become millionaires than native residents. These new arrivals begin by leaving behind their security, heritage, family and friends, and everything that is comfortable and familiar to them. In hopes that they are traveling to a place with much greater opportunity, they may start out with very little but sense there is so much they can gain. Because they are starting out in survival mode, they often establish a sound work ethic that carries through when new opportunities present themselves.

During a trip to Tanzania, I remember being fascinated by many of the large animals that one can expect to see on the plains of the Serengeti. To see elephants and giraffes roaming in the wild was surreal, but an equally intriguing moment was to witness how gazelles seem to fly with each jump, as they remained airborne for quite some distance. When I asked our guide if it was documented just how far they could leap, I was astounded to learn that not only could they jump ten feet in height, but also a distance of sixty feet.

My eyes weren't deceiving me when they seemed to glide through the air forever. When I thought back to visiting an assortment of zoos in the States as a youngster, something didn't quite add up. I remember seeing these same sleek animals in an area that only had a four-foot fence. So if they could jump so high, why didn't they just leap out of their pen to freedom? My guide then explained that a gazelle won't jump if it can't see where it's going to land. Therefore, a low fence was sufficient to keep them from taking a chance on something they couldn't see. My biggest fear in heli-skiing the Canadian Rockies was the constant warnings about avalanches. Had I known before I went that our guide had lost ten skiers the previous year, I probably would have elected to stay at home.

Too many times we misinterpret a small risk as taking a big chance, and we're afraid to jump at something if we're not one hundred percent sure where we're going to land. In the same way we learn to make better decisions by making more of them, we can also learn to take better risks by taking more of them, too. The easiest way to practice is to take fun risks with fewer consequences so when it becomes imperative to take a critical risk, it won't feel quite as foreign to us.

Life is automatic; living is the result of risk, trust, and change.

I recall taking a rather humorous risk when the stakes were high, at least as far as a valuable friendship goes. A good friend of mine from Penn State was getting married and asked me to be one of his ushers. His bride-to-be came from an affluent family who was obviously concerned about everything being perfect for their daughter's special day. During the rehearsal, I could already feel the level of anxiety rising as so much pressure is always placed on the one shot chance for everything to be perfect in front of friends and relatives.

Before I left for the wedding, I went to a locksmith and persuaded him to give me a couple hundred old keys from locks he had changed, knowing that he would probably just discard them anyway. I divided the keys among the other ushers and told them not to mention a word. Then as we ushered all the attendees into the church on the wedding day, each woman was inconspicuously handed a key and instructed to keep it a secret until they were asked to return it.

The wedding went just as planned, but, with so many visitors from out of town, there was still a degree of tension as the reception began. Before the meal, the groom's brother stood up and offered a very thoughtful and tasteful toast. When he finished, I immediately took the microphone from him, much to the bride's parents' surprise, as this was not part of the rehearsal. "I've known Ted for quite some time now," I announced. "And during those years he's dated a lot of very fine women, although today he has resigned himself to just one. So if any of you ladies, by chance, still have a key to one of his former apartments, could you please bring it up to him now?"

Instantly the room became dead silent, and I could feel a strong sense of hesitation. The next few seconds seemed like minutes, as many people looked to the bride's parents in shock. Then suddenly, one by one, every woman with a key began approaching the head table and dropping the keys in front of the groom. Initially many people not in on my prank looked appalled, but as the women kept coming up in droves, the facial expressions turned to laughter, and, for the first time, the atmosphere in the entire room became exceptionally relaxed.

I had even given keys out to the staff at the restaurant; and the older invited guests, especially, couldn't wait to participate. They were all anxious to become a part of this spontaneous farce. What could have been a disastrous misunderstanding became a turning point in breaking the ice and making their celebration more memorable.

So where do we begin in learning how to think differently? The first and most important step, as mentioned earlier, is to place a higher amount of trust into any of our own ideas. Too often we disregard them as not being plausible and worthwhile. Then how do we create that self-confidence and substantiate that even our simplest thoughts are deserving of consideration?

An optimal starting point is to let our natural curiosity take over and develop a stronger sense of wonder. We are instilled with wonder as children but become increasingly calloused over time. We may talk about it or even describe it, but we should strive to make our inquisitiveness more emotional. By trusting our own intuition and developing a constant thirst for understanding why things are the way they are, and why this or that isn't possible, we will prevent short-circuiting one of our greatest capacities.

**Always keep
your mind open
to possibility.**

Everyone has a story to tell. We all have a book inside of us. Every individual possesses a unique way of sharing information with someone else. The way to jumpstart our enthusiasm is to genuinely see ourselves as being the only person on the planet who can interpret something exactly as we do, which is the truth.

There's a long handed down story about Socrates' peculiar manner of teaching a student how to develop his own enthusiasm. One day a young boy approached Socrates on a beach and inquired, "How can I increase my desire to learn?" For several moments, Socrates just sat there as though he hadn't even heard the request. Then he stood up and walked into the water.

The boy followed. Socrates kept walking deeper into the water, and the boy continued to follow him. Finally Socrates grabbed the top of his head and forced him underneath the surface. He held his head there, completely submerged, so that the boy wasn't able to breathe.

The young lad struggled and fought to get away, pushing him and fighting for his life.

After a very short time, the boy finally gave up as his arms lay limp from exhaustion. Only then did Socrates lift his head out of the water, while the young boy began gasping for air. Still coughing and choking he screamed, "Why did you do that? Don't you realize I almost drowned? All I did was ask you a question. How could that possibly help me to learn anything?"

Then Socrates finally replied, "When you develop a passion for what you desire to learn, as greatly as the one you just had when you wanted to breathe, only then will you receive the knowledge you so desperately want to acquire."

Fortunately there are also other ways to generate enthusiasm. When we drive somewhere familiar to us, it's instinctual to take the shortest known route. One common way to stimulate our imagination is to occasionally take a less efficient road, one that reveals sights and landscapes we don't typically see. While more time consuming, consider the possibilities of an alternative mode of travel. So, why would you ever want to take a train or a bus if you have the convenience of your own car?

This will sound completely senseless to many people because who has that amount of time to devote to slower commuting? Ironically, many of us will spend hundreds of dollars going to seminars and trying to buy all the right books, hoping to achieve something that we can also accomplish on our own once we agree to think in terms of possibility. How can we expect to learn something new if all we do is repeatedly expose ourselves to things we already know?

To stretch your imagination even further than an indirect route, consider hiking, taking a ferry, riding a bicycle, or simply walking somewhere new during your spare time. It's not just about exercise or taking your mind off work. Changing what's already recognizable to you can rejuvenate your thought process, even while concentrating on work or making important decisions. Speed may be the most efficient way of doing, but it is not the most effective way of learning. When we slow things down to a more palatable pace, we'll notice things impossible to see during the blur of our routine lives.

When the laptop is closed and we're detached from our work, we have infinite choices for novel recreation that help tremendously in refreshing the way we think. If we look inside the word *recreation*, we find *re - create*, which defines what we're trying to do. We want to reinvent ourselves for the moment, to get away from our mundane rituals. When we want to play... as a response to our increased level of activity, our mind is more likely to play, too. By keeping our eyes open, we can make unexpected discoveries especially while being active.

The beginning of knowledge is the discovery of something that we don't understand.

One of the most peaceful and hypnotic forms of recreation I've ever found has been scuba diving. While suspended in water with a true sense of weightlessness, where the only sound is that of my own breathing through a regulator, it's the closest experience I can imagine to being on the moon. The buoyancy created by the water provides an incredibly dreamlike feeling that cannot be duplicated.

If someone is not that adventurous or doesn't have the time to engage in a sport that requires a certain amount of training, there are easier ways to simulate an unusual environment. It can be as simple as closing your ears so you can listen to the haunting sound of your own breathing as it resonates inside your head. Or, do the opposite and try closing your eyes while listening for noises that you normally wouldn't recognize. The more adept you are at creating an artificial environment for yourself, the greater chance you have of altering where your mind goes.

From my experience, one of the best ways to stimulate our thinking is by traveling to an unfamiliar destination. Travel helps us to revitalize and provides a fresh viewpoint that we may not have appreciated before. When we go somewhere new we are less likely to have specific expectations about what we'll find. Refusing to stay in a chain hotel or eating food we can easily find at home will undoubtedly help us to detoxify from the stereotypical routine that we already know. Explore the possibility of a bed and breakfast, public transportation, or trust the recommendations of the locals. It may be most beneficial *not* to do too much planning. It's great to have a skeleton itinerary, but leave enough time that you can be open to the outcome.

One of the more unconventional trips I have ever taken began by planning not to plan. I had scheduled a week away from work and had a predetermined amount of money I was willing to spend. I intentionally made no prior arrangements, and decided I would take advantage of any last minute travel deal available, forcing myself to have less control and throwing any expectations to the wind. With the popularity of Websites like Travelocity and Expedia, you can always find great value seats on unfilled flights and available rooms on cruise ships. At the eleventh hour, I stumbled upon a very inexpensive flight to Lisbon.

The only advance preparation I made was to purchase a travel book about Portugal the night before leaving as well as to pack a week's worth of clothing for my spontaneous adventure. It can be both taxing and exhilarating to land in a country where you can't speak the language and have no itinerary whatsoever.

Every major airport in Europe has a helpful tourist information center, and the one in Lisbon did a credible job of directing me to the tiny village of Sintra, about an hour outside the city. This little jewel of a town with a lost-in-the-past feel was one of the highest points in the area and an archetypal setting for allowing my mind to escape. When we travel to unusual locations, especially places we happen upon haphazardly, our minds have the luxury of enjoying all of our senses in a novel way.

Each world culture has its own characteristics and unique ways for dealing with life day to day. What seems commonplace for them can seem uncanny to an outsider. The first time I flew on Aeroflot, one of the largest airlines in the world and based in the Russian Federation, I was shocked to find cats and dogs (and an array of other farm animals) freely running about the cabin. During a portion of the flight they even wandered in and around my legs. When the No Smoking sign lit up (in English) it was as if it were a signal for everyone on the plane to light up. Not one person other than my travel partner and me wore a seatbelt during that entire flight. The continuous loud rattling of unlatched doors and the ill sounding engines made me overly concerned about how long it had been since the plane was last serviced.

During another travel stint, while in some of the most remote parts of India, I learned why it is not appropriate to ever offer or receive something (especially a handshake) with your left hand. Because many of these areas are still quite poverty-stricken and don't have the convenience of toilet paper, it is customary to clean yourself with the left hand. Any means of exchange between people is, therefore, out of sanitary courtesy always shared with the right hand.

Before setting off on foot into the depths of the Amazon jungle, among some of the deadliest plants and animals in the world, it was customary to visit the local witch doctor.

Throughout his "good luck" ceremony, we were instructed to drink a potion that had been especially prepared for my friend Rob and me. This was considered a generous gift from several local women who had been chewing on the roots of plants all day and then spitting the juices into an urn. In this case, out of respect for them and caution for ourselves, we gave the illusion that we were partaking of their kind offering. I wish I could say the same during the latter part of the week when we succumbed to eating larva, that were still alive and crawling, as part of our balanced diet.

Not traveling to explore our world is like living in the Library of Congress, yet never reading.

It's not until we place ourselves quite a distance from where we live that we can begin to capture an essence of how the world is perceived from the eyes of a real stranger. When we truly want to push our perspective to its limits, traveling can offer a renewed appreciation for other people's point of reference, which can ultimately affect our own frame of mind. Removing ourselves from the confines of what we already know offers an incomparable opportunity to reflect.

Nature's Calling

There's another opportune place to stimulate our thinking except it's so invisible to us it is seldom ever noticed. Hidden within nature all around us are some of the most perfect examples of biochemistry and physics that can invoke our imagination. The annoyance of an unwanted spider web can be readily swiped away without a second thought. When we take a moment to examine the complexity of this seemingly fragile structure, we discover that not only does it have remarkable flexibility and resistance to the elements, its tensile strength is superior to that of high-grade steel.

Another example of nature's thought provoking mysteries are the barnacles that commonly attach themselves to the underside of a boat. For a boat owner, they can represent a nightmare of labor, but consider that this creature has an inherent glue that not only works under water, it also adheres better and longer than almost any commercially manufactured glue.

A creature that most people are swift to avoid but should incite an inventive mind is the snake. By studying their unique ocular proficiencies, which allow them to see well at night, scientists have been able to use the information as the basis for developing various types of infrared technology. From some of the latest improvements in photography, to the most advanced seeking devices in the armed forces, and even the newer techno games, this discovered adaptation of nature has been slithering beneath us for thousands of years.

As you are probably well aware, the innermost depths of the Amazon jungle are a goldmine for an ever-increasing number of medicinal products. Many unusual plants and animals found here are either a primary source of ingredients for pharmaceutical companies directly or, otherwise, act as the basis for synthetic products that can be reproduced in a laboratory. It's amazing how many technology-related intricacies there are disguised within nature and what they have to offer when we take the time to look.

When it comes to "human" nature, we are often guilty of working against ourselves. We can take advantage of a much faster learning curve when we are willing to work in unity. We've become a nation of independence, which cyberspace has only furthered, yet the more often we share our thought process with others, the more likely we are to expand our own thinking. In working with many businesses, I still find that one of the prime roadblocks in limiting their success is the essentials of teamwork. Society is predisposed to embracing self-sufficiency. When co-workers are open-minded about each other's thoughts, it creates a powerful environment filled with potential. As people become more dependent on each other, especially in trying situations, they also become more directed toward a common success.

One of my favorite more adventurous activities for developing a sense of teamwork and inter-dependency is having a company take their employees rock climbing. While it may look intimidating and dangerous, it's actually very safe (even more so when practicing on an artificial surface indoors). There's probably a greater risk of twisting your ankle while walking to the climb than getting hurt while you're "tied in" to the rock. Even though you are solely responsible for your own upward movement, you cannot descend or fall downwards without the assistance of your climbing partner. The strategy is to find the easiest "holds" while using the least amount of effort.

Most men have greater upper body strength than women do and are prone to using it in pulling themselves upward. This is quite deceiving as it will tire you much more rapidly. Women, on the other hand, have a natural tendency to use their legs as much as possible, which is also the smartest way to climb. This brief escape from the office has proven to be an extraordinary self-motivator for overcoming fears and learning to trust both yourself and your teammate. After reaching the top of an exhilarating climb, suddenly the paperwork back in the office seems easily surmountable.

If we don't do something that scares on occasion, we're not testing our abilities adequately. We each have our own fear factor level that we bring to the table. Overcoming these fears in a physical way can translate well to the office. Suddenly, when we return, our mind is racing with ideas after an adventure that rekindled our spirit and offered us a new perspective.

We should always be on the lookout for both simple and adventurous ways to see our world from a unique standpoint. If we have a practice of entering the private rear entrance to our office, maybe we need to walk in the front door next time, the same way our customers do. By never resorting to this, we may not be in tune with the experience that everyone else receives upon entering and, again, not learn from placing ourselves inside someone else's head. Sometimes simply changing the décor in a room or interchanging small responsibilities among the staff can be motivating in itself. Any way we can get our minds to approach the same work from a new angle has the likelihood of offering new insight.

The most exciting phrase to hear in science along the road to discovery is not "eureka," but rather "that's funny."

A friend of mine shared a story about an atypical theatrical instructor who teaches in New York City. His students had memorized the lines to *Romeo and Juliet* so they could rehearse without a script in their hands. Having read the lines so many times, it became harder for them to sense the emotion they required to deliver the lines with real passion. He needed a way for them to feel the true obsession and infatuation of what it was like to be in the moment.

He selected two students to play the main characters and divided the rest of the class in half. The actors were placed about five feet apart. Half the class was instructed to tightly hold the arms and legs of one actor while the other half hung onto the arms and legs of the other. The actors were now told to read their scripts again, but at the same time they were supposed to struggle to get free so they could touch each other.

They read all the same lines once more, but this time they were physically fighting to get closer to the other person during the entire scene. They frantically pushed and shoved, doing anything possible to reach the other person. For the first time, they read each line with so much incentive and intensity that they actually sounded entirely different.

After nearly fifteen minutes of struggling to the point of near exhaustion, the instructor told the two teams to let them go. Finally finding themselves unrestrained, the actors reached each other's arms and delivered their lines to each other with more emotion and sincerity than ever before.

> **One of the best ways to discover something new is to play.** —Albert Einstein

To this day I am still fascinated by my memories of tossing out plastic necklaces from a parade float during Gasparillo, which is Tampa's version of Mardi Gras. People from all walks of life would crowd around every float while desperately scrambling for the plastic beads being thrown, as though they were made of gold. In the same way that Disney World can disarm our maturity and restore our thrills as a child, for one short hour nothing seemed to matter more than collecting those bright colored beads. Amid this festive event, I witnessed everyone from grandmothers with their grandchildren to some of the highest paid professionals collecting necklaces and divorcing their daily facade to enjoy this rambunctious opportunity to play.

Whether it's embracing our natural instincts to play or discovering a lost part of nature around us, one goal that we should continually strive to achieve is to release ourselves from any confining molds and discover more of what we are made of.

Visually Impaired

As mentioned at the very beginning of this book, our vision collects the majority of sensory information we receive. We also know by removing one of our five senses, some of the others will become keener to make up for our loss. By toying with our imagination, we can explore interconnecting biases of how our mind's eye interprets what we see.

Many artists and design professionals use an escapism technique to help remove themselves from the accepted norm. For instance, try to "draw" a particular sound you hear. Or describe the way a particular food tastes by only using numbers. Can you use nothing more than colors to express what type of mood you're experiencing? How would you depict a recent travel adventure using only items found in your kitchen? By tapping your senses in a very unorthodox manner, you change the context of how you use them, which forces you to think differently.

Most of us as adults just don't play enough. We can take life much too seriously and neglect to challenge our senses enough throughout the day to make living more fun and stimulating. It may take nothing more than a little humor or a trivial puzzle to take our routine pattern of thinking away from a treadmill of work and into a mindset of innovative problem solving. The Internet or any bookstore can offer a wide variety of brainteasers appropriate for a quick fix mental break, which can help to get our gears turning. Here are a few samples I've shared with groups in the past. The first one dates back to something an art teacher taught us in fourth grade.

By taking the Roman numeral seven and adding one line to it, we could create an eight.

Likewise, by removing one line from the Roman numeral nine, we could create a ten.

But is it possible to add a one line to the Roman numeral nine to create a six? Think for a moment before turning the page to see if you're right.

SIX

Most people assume the "single line" must be straight. But that drastically limits our thinking... anytime we make an assumption.

Here's another one, known as the Mobius strip, to test your imagination. Use a newspaper or a large piece of scrap paper to cut out a long narrow strip similar to the one in the figure on right. (This experiment will be easier to demonstrate if you use a much longer strip of the same width than the one shown.) Bring the ends together and either tape or glue them so that you have a perfect ring with no twists. (The notches at the ends of the strip create a starting point for your scissors to cut in the next step.) Now try cutting midway around the entire ring to create two rings of the same circumference that are only half as wide.

You could have easily predicted exactly what these two rings would look like before you ever cut them, but this was an important action in helping you to understand the next two steps. Now cut another strip the same size as the last, but before fastening the ends together give one of the ends a half twist. Before you cut midway around the entire circumference again, can you predict what will happen this time? (Take a few moments to try and guess exactly what the outcome will be.) You will find the result very startling, but it gets even better. Make one last strip, but this time give one end a full twist before attaching the ends. Again, try to imagine what will happen to the strips when you complete the cut. It is this type of theoretical thinking (even when we guess *wrong*) that can take our minds to new and improbable places.

The next exercise is ideal for a larger group when wanting to expose how our minds can become hostage to our memories. Ask everyone to create a paper airplane from a single eight and a half by eleven-inch sheet of paper. Challenge them to fold the paper into any design they like, possibly even more aerodynamic than the example in the sample illustration. Who in the group can create an aircraft that will fly the greatest distance?

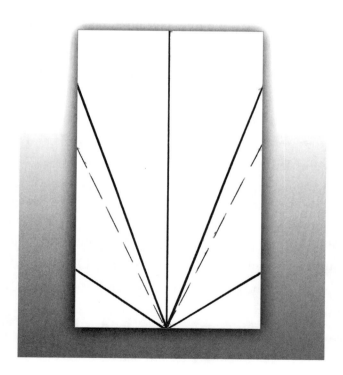

After every person has launched their own creation and you've measured the longest distance, demonstrate the design of your own aircraft. Remind them, again, that the only requirement was to fold a single sheet of paper into whatever shape they could to make it travel the greatest distance. Now simply crumple your sheet into a tight little ball and whip it as far as possible across the room. Yours will undoubtedly travel the farthest since its compact weight is no match for any air resistance against the others. Our preconceived notions tell us our paper should resemble something with wings and a pointed nose. But, when not given any limitations about how it should look and the ways it can be projected, the typical paper airplane that we grew up with becomes comparatively much less flight worthy.

The reason these distractive puzzles can be helpful at work is that today we've become accustomed to living in an entertainment economy. Entertainment touches all facets of our lives, from the way we communicate to the way we respond as consumers. As a society, we expect and even demand to be entertained if you want to hold our attention. This does not imply we are all couch potatoes or we will lose our focus on what's important. It's just that we've found it's possible to still have fun while working, learning, keeping fit, and even fulfilling responsibilities that are somewhat monotonous. All the media and marketing surrounding us has decidedly demonstrated we prefer making buying decisions and longer commitments when we're in a pleasure oriented frame of mind.

Business meetings are also more effective and productive when they are interactive, playful, and thought provoking. When we want to keep people's minds from wandering and becoming dissociated during this valuable time, we need to compete with the stimulation they receive from activities outside the office. How can we encourage attendees to become more involved and take an active role in making a meeting more productive? When personalities become predictable and people feel trapped in an organizational rut, what "off the wall" forms of playing can revitalize a narrow way of thinking?

In order to cradle people's attention and get them actively involved, a meeting has to be eventful. It doesn't have to be elaborately themed to be successful; it only has to be entertain*ing*, without being entertain*ment*.

Not long ago I helped a business to create an innovative and memorable summit by having them assign each of fifteen people a different foreign accent for the first five minutes of the session. Not only did this lend to a much lighter atmosphere, but it aided in trying to release a hidden persona inside some of them. By giving them the freedom to act out of character, they actually felt different, too. This works in the same way that karaoke singing can reveal a hidden thirst for stardom in someone who's typically more introverted.

At the very least, we can gain a hint of enthusiasm for every gathering by simply adding an interesting theme element. It doesn't have to be elaborate, and the more abstract the better. For instance, is there anyone working for you that is thirty-one and a half years old? At this point you have two more months to prepare for the big day. When they reach thirty-one years and eight months, why not throw a "billion seconds party" for him or her? (It takes that long to live a billion seconds of our life.) If you really hit a mental block for ideas consider hiring a meeting planner, as this is their specialty, but it's not too hard to be creative on your own.

Try to imagine what Steven Spielberg would do if he were in your office and designing a function for you. What might he cleverly bring to the table to ensure that everyone was excited about participating? How would he redesign the seating arrangement, or a protocol that allows everyone to contribute equally? How would he create a sense of mystery to a discussion, while still guaranteeing that the attendees remember the focus of why they are there?

What would be an approach that Blue Man Group might incorporate to assure more spontaneity and make your meeting more unforgettable? If the think tank from Cirque de Soleil were in charge of hosting your business meeting, what simple yet stunning ideas might they come up with?

There are no rules, except that we are trying to accomplish something.
—Thomas Edison

Earlier in these pages there was a reference made to reverse thinking, which is one of the most insightful ways to fire up our unexploited brain cells. Corporate America is, now more than ever, concerned about practicality and streamlining while also saving time and money. An excellent exercise for opening new frontiers is to temporarily imagine the most expensive way to accomplish something, or the most time consuming way to carry it out, or the least practical way to achieve your goal. Instead of doing something the easy way, what would make it the most demanding and complicated way? Which way would be the most childish and nonsensical, or most stressful, or most energy intense? Obviously we don't want to end up here, but this has proven to be a profitable exercise for diverting us from traditional thinking. Later, after refining something that may first appear outlandish, it may unpredictably turn into a very practical and cost-effective idea.

My interest in illusions has also proven to be very beneficial in seeing things from an unlikely perspective. I've also found it to be a very effective tool for engaging people's curiosity and promoting a team approach to problem solving. An illusionist always assumes that anything is accomplishable. The only question is in determining which of infinite possibilities will provide the desired outcome most effectively. By setting up small groups around a room and having them master a simple magical puzzle (within as little as a ten-minute time period) to present to the entire group, an exciting and expansive energy will often surface that can spill into the rest of the gathering.

One example of a simple sleight of hand feat that can be easily taught is the "two-headed quarter." Place a quarter, heads up, on top of your open fingers, about half an inch from your fingertips. If you turn your hand over and slap the coin down on a table, it will obviously land tails side up. But, you can learn how to mimic the exact same movement and still have it land heads side up, once you master a secret move.

Start with the coin at the original position near your fingertips, but this time you're going to momentarily bend your fingers toward yourself to turn the coin over, before your entire hand is turned to slap it on the table. Practice this very slowly at first; you'll soon realize that you can also do this very smoothly and imperceptibly, so there's no detection by your audience. The larger movement of your hand turning over masks the smaller movement of your fingers bending. It will appear as though you did nothing more than just slap the coin down the way you did before. However, the coin now appears to have a head on both sides.

As you become more proficient at this, you can control which side of the coin is up on the table just by whether you bend your fingers or not. It may still seem apparent to you, but it won't be noticeable to anyone else. You can even make this a competitive team effort to see who can master it most deceptively.

Both the theatrical arts and fine arts have a way of setting us free from our perpetual mind traps. An opportune way to exercise our brains is to delve a little deeper into any aspect of the arts that we have an affinity to explore... even if it's just as an observer.

Raising Our Eye Q

It's easy to get stuck in our heads and become complacent among the myriad of responsibilities that fight for our attention every day. Almost paradoxically, just when we try to expand our thinking, everyday life seems to encapsulate us and restrain us from reaching new plateaus. Any form of leverage that facilitates breaking away from our boring consistencies should be openly welcomed.

My favorite people to interact with are both optimistic and opportunistic. We all have challenging moments, primary concerns, and important issues that require our attention on a daily basis. But even in the midst of life's adversities, we can choose our own attitude and can focus on the best we can do within the confines of what we have to work with.

I was only going thirty miles per hour while plodding through the center of my home town, when suddenly a drunk driver slammed into the right side of my new car and forced me to hit another car parked on the left side of me. If that wasn't enough, after he glanced off my vehicle and plowed into a different parked car than the one I had hit, he then threw his car into reverse and nailed me a third time before speeding off down the road.

Thankfully, due to his slow speed of travel and because the major impact occurred on the passenger side of the car, I was not hurt at all. Within seconds many bystanders who had witnessed the accident came to check if I was alright.

"He just hit your new car," someone said. "Talk about ruining your day."

At that very moment, I looked across the street and noticed a young girl in a wheelchair. So with the least sense of anger I immediately decided, no... it's actually a pretty good day.

As an eye doctor, I occasionally deal with life-altering diseases and sight-threatening conditions. I inevitably try to create a balance between addressing important concerns and still keeping patients smiling and seeing the brighter aspects of any situation.

The more compassionate we can be in focusing on desired outcomes, the stronger our rapport will be and the better we will connect with others. Our ability to focus on the positive, under *any* circumstances, can go a long way toward cementing a lasting relationship.

Ben Underwood suffered a complication known as bilateral retinoblastoma (cancerous tumors in each eye) that left him blind in both eyes since the age of two. Each eye had to be removed the following year. However, his mother was exceptionally encouraging and made him smile at what most people would accept as sorrowful. By the age of five Ben discovered that by making a clicking noise with his mouth, he was able to locate most objects in his immediate surroundings, much in the way dolphins use echolocation to do the same.

By the time he was a teenager, he could skate safely on the sidewalks of his street, and even sense the difference between a trashcan and a fire hydrant that might be in his path. His capabilities were almost miraculous and even documented on national news broadcasts.

Without any sight, he would have pillow fights with his siblings and was more accurate than they were when it came to hitting a moving target. In the face of great adversity, he has proven that the human spirit can conquer almost any misfortune, when given the right motivation. (Sadly, Ben recently succumbed to the same cancer that had stolen his eyesight.)

Live on the outer edge of possibility, not the inner edge of security.

I am continually astonished by man's capacity to overcome great odds. When we experience limitations in one phase of our lives, it's usually possible to compensate and resort to our other strengths. So it stands to reason if we're willing to attempt this "artificially," maybe other hidden talents will present themselves. There are actually services within the military and even adventure travel companies that offer specialized training in how to survive a disastrous situation, such as an earthquake or a plane crash. As only one illustration, by securely taping your hands into a tightly closed fist to simulate what you may have to endure as a burn victim, you might discover that you can rely on your arms or legs in an entirely new fashion. The preeminent way to develop a new product, especially for someone who is compromised, is to place ourselves in the same situation.

If our imagination was at its peak as a child, then resorting to child-like diversions could be a trigger that enhances our ability to dream. Actually, these can be the very moments that allow us to push our creativity to its maximum heights, which is why they should be given strong consideration. This will seldom work by merely staying in our heads... it requires active participation.

While we can try to imagine what it's like to run a marathon, it's impossible to truly understand the amount of discipline, relentless training, or mind games athletes endure (such as runner's block just miles from the finish line) until we physically do it ourselves. The same is true for the following exercises. Only *thinking* about how you might feel offers no comparison to how you might be moved when experiencing something *physically*.

Some of the simplest tools at our disposal can change the way we see things forever. For instance, an aerial view of our work area can yield surprising results. Use a chair or a stepladder (or even a balcony when possible) to access a different vantage point than what you're accustomed to seeing, and try to evaluate what you see from this new perspective.

Suppose we were watching an NFL football game from a blimp, and the movement of the football itself was the only thing we were tracking and recording. The entire game would now be reduced to a series of lines that go back and forth, representing the path of the ball on a finite field. By eliminating the players, the fans, all the noise and adrenaline, we break down the essence of what's important (the ball reaching one of the end zones) into its most basic form. So how can we apply this same philosophy to our work situation?

Maybe better than elevating ourselves in tandem with a bird's eye view, is to make a recording at this higher level. It then becomes possible to evaluate what we see over an extended period of time. This is not meant as a spying device for someone else as much as a method to see ourselves from a point of view we never have the chance to experience. I spoke with a CEO who tried this and found several ways to make himself more proficient and relaxed. By overseeing the way he interacted with others, he not only made an internal character change but was able to modify his abruptness in dealing with others and see the larger picture of what he wanted his business to symbolize. The key was in trying something physically different to see a new perspective.

If we drop something as small as a contact lens on the floor, it can be extremely difficult to find standing up. On the contrary, if we lower ourselves to place our eyes as close to the floor as possible, we have a much better chance of seeing its projection above the flat surface it's resting on. This is similar to a golfer who bends down to evaluate the contour of the green before his or her next putt. Opening our minds to new perspectives may entail having to physically raise or lower our eyes to an unthinkable plane.

To make better sense of the illustration on the next page, it will help to raise the book so that your eyes are horizontal with the bottom of that page.

There are numerous ways to modify our perspective without ever leaving our chair. In one instance during a brief meeting, the session leader was concerned about having everyone's full attention. He wanted to eliminate the chance his employees would continually be stealing glimpses of their messages. So I suggested placing one-inch black circles (plastic tape) in the middle of the lenses of everyone's glasses during the entire meeting. (He provided the attendees who didn't wear glasses inexpensive ones with no prescription and the same black circles.)

This created a very fascinating environment for every attendee. For the first time during a meeting, they couldn't see the eyes of the person who was speaking, and were, therefore, much more focused on what they were saying (as well as not knowing if that person was even looking at them). More importantly, when diagrams and charts were referred to during the discussion, they were forced to use their imagination to fill in part of the missing picture. Their visual clues were strictly limited to their periphery.

Our perception can be influenced more by what we don't see, than what we really see.

This actually resulted in a more intricate involvement of the participants with more questions being asked, due to the greater number of challenges. It ultimately produced a better understanding of the concept being presented by the time the meeting was over. Needless to say, they devoted more attention than usual, which was instigated by creating an obstacle rather than eliminating one.

When a patient has a strabismus (the misalignment of the eyes in which one eye deviates inward or outward), their condition can sometimes be improved with eye exercises. These were referred to earlier and are known as visual therapy. An interesting phenomenon can be employed to give them the experience of binocularity, when both eyes function equally as a team. It is accomplished with the use of a balance board.

Using a twenty-four inch square piece of plywood, the narrow edge of a twenty-four inch two-by-four is then attached to the middle of the underside. It's a fairly easy task for anyone to step onto the board and balance it to a level point, making it parallel to the floor. But to keep it in that position as we maintain our balance, our body must rely on the brain's vestibular apparatus, and the eyes of a strabismus patient will often straighten simultaneously.

I have seen many occasions in which this is the very first time in a patient's life that their eyes line up straight and they experience binocular vision. Obviously they can't spend eternity on a balance board, but this is an initial step in allowing them to understand how the proper alignment of their eyes should feel as they continue their visual training process.

In the same way, by standing on a balance board ourselves, as our brain reacts to our physical stimulus for balance, it can also affect and modify our way of thinking. Changing how we feel physically alters the way we construct our thoughts both mentally and emotionally. Once you've reached a sense of stability on the board which is learned rather quickly, gently close your eyes (various yoga positions can accomplish the same prerequisite for balance). You'll be amazed at how this very slight amount of physical exertion removes some of the roadblocks to expanded thinking.

From basic optical principles, you are probably already familiar with the concept that a convex lens will magnify an object while a concave lens will reduce an object's apparent size. A comparative way to examine this for yourself is with a pair of binoculars. Using them the correct way will magnify your subject while making it appear closer than it actually is. Turning them around and looking through them backwards will reduce the subject size while making it appear much further away.

Both of these viewpoints can be beneficial for intentionally distorting the way we normally see things. Our preemptive thinking reminds us that binoculars were invented to assist our vision at a sports event or help us locate wildlife. But using them within the confines of a room or even close up not only restricts our peripheral vision to a single point of focus, but may help us to notice or appreciate something valuable that would not have been obvious otherwise.

In the same way that each of us learns differently, we also use our vision differently, too. Try giving a friend or coworker your cell phone or camera and having them take several pictures in a nearby area, either close up or in a way that the subject is indefinable. You would surely recognize any of the objects in their entirety, but with only a glimpse of the whole picture and being unsure of what you see, it can help to change the way you interpret what's around you.

Genius is only a superior power of seeing. —John Ruskin

One day while taking flying lessons, I was given a special pair of goggles to wear after my instructor and I were in flight. The special lenses blocked the top half of my vision so I could no longer see through any window. This standard procedure during flight training forces the student pilot to rely solely on the instruments for navigating the aircraft. It was an ideal method of building my confidence in the event of inclement weather.

A variation of this same concept can be used in any type of environment by modifying our field of view. By temporarily eliminating outside distractions from a certain direction, we can funnel our attention onto one specific area or portion of a project without interference from our side vision. This can be beneficial in particular instances when it's adamant to control our focus.

The beginning of this book demonstrated the way in which a mirror can be extremely deceptive. Illusionists have a long history of using mirrors to intentionally distort our belief in what we actually see. Mirrors equally allow us to use distortion to our advantage, too. A full wall mirror in a small restaurant can make patrons feel less claustrophobic (or make us curious as to where the person being reflected is actually seated).

Don't overlook the possibilities of using a mirror, or multiple mirrors, either above, below, or beside an area requiring your attention when you become complacent in how to interpret what you see. Again, your first reaction will be that the outcome is too easy to imagine rather than going to any trouble and expense. Except, beyond just being reflective, a mirror has characteristics that are difficult to predict. Any illusionist will tell you that some of the special effects possible, even in this millennium, are nothing less than spectacular. The small investment of time and money may pay for itself many times over.

20/20 Listening

The practice of brainstorming dates back to ancient Greece, long before the word itself was ever coined. What I find most fascinating, though, are the rules and guidelines that the participants agreed to abide by whenever they took part in one of these creative discussions. One principle strictly adhered to was that no one was ever allowed to argue or disagree while someone else was elaborating on their thoughts and insight. The goal was to not interrupt and to listen carefully. They well respected how much more they could learn by listening rather than speaking.

I have witnessed countless brainstorming sessions within a wide variety of businesses in which the attendees become uncommonly judgmental before an idea is even fully explained, let alone explored. In some instances, people are so impatient that they blurt out, "No, I know from experience your idea would never work here." Or, "We've tried that before and it never gets off the ground." And, "Our corporate office would never justify the expense for your idea. It's just not practical."

The ancient Greeks taught us that everyone should have an equal say in creativity and we should never cloud someone's vision when he or she is attempting to express an idea. At one Fortune 500 company's think tank session, we handed out Nerf balls emphasizing that the participants should not take these ancient methods too lightly.

Anytime that someone made a derogatory comment or displayed a negative attitude, especially when new suggestions were offered, the others were instructed to bombard the individual with direct shots to the body. The meeting turned out to be more productive and more fun, and it didn't take long until everyone got the message. The participants began to speak more freely and with less concern that their ideas would be shot down.

This book is about our vision; not about becoming an "I" specialist. It seems a bit incongruous that society keeps encouraging us to be more independent when we don't typically function to our highest capacity that way. Parents usually feel as though they have accomplished their responsibility when their children finally become self-sufficient. Yet, we are typically more excitable, productive, and fulfilled through the synergy of other people. If we share the right chemistry with someone else, our potential increases dramatically. This is ultimately why people hire coaches and trainers. We all benefit from a support team or an individual who can help to maintain our focus on our goals.

Penn State and Notre Dame are the only two college football teams that don't put the individual names of the players on their jerseys. This is because Joe Paterno and Charlie Weiss want to emphasize that winning can only be accomplished as a team effort. I know personally from friends of mine that played under Paterno that he is not quick to judge. He advocates impartiality and treats all of his athletes equally. This should also hold true in any meaningful think tank session. As a cooperative effort, everyone should genuinely be given an equal opportunity to offer his or her thoughts. It's often the case that some of the best ideas will come from the least likely people.

I often refer to these no-limit thought sessions as "cloud sessions" implying that the sky is the limit, and strongly reinforce that the only danger is in pre-judging someone's idea too quickly. When you don't limit your imagination, you won't limit your success. Let your imagination run as far as it can.

**Only those who
risk going too far
will know how far
they can go.**

As much as we make a serious effort in wanting to think differently, sometimes we just hit the wall. We try not to limit our thoughts, but just can't seem to get beyond where our minds have been before. One of the most empowering ways to not only enhance our own depth of knowledge but to expand our thinking as well is to teach something.

It's hard to instruct another person without first knowing the subject adequately ourselves. Since each person will learn differently, teaching multiple people gives us the opportunity to offer multiple types of answers to their unique questions. This, in turn, presents a variety of perspectives as we continue to modify the way we see things in the process. An important step is to sit back and "listen to what we've just said" to someone else. This can be dually rewarding in that it helps us assimilate alternative ways to approach learning, too.

Another valuable exercise is to explain or talk about our thoughts out loud rather than simply scribbling them down or just mulling over them silently. Even when no one else is present, asking a question vocally or describing your thoughts with enthusiasm (much like an actor rehearsing) may help you become more aware of an idea that could have been lost. I sometimes refer to this process as "the invisible shrink."

When you don't have the opportunity to actually speak with another person about your ideas or the decisions you want to make, try to imagine you're paying five hundred dollars an hour for a professional consultant (who is not plainly visible). You'll be surprised by the amount of advice you receive just by listening to yourself out loud. The key is in remembering to press yourself with questions someone else might likely ask you. Forcing yourself to become more specific can be enough to guide you in new directions.

Alternatively, it can also be a great exercise to imagine yourself trying to explain something to another person with only the use of pictures. Instead of speaking, limit yourself to a camera or cell phone to take an array of photos used to depict the concept you want to translate to someone else. You may be amazed at how differently you approach the same intended outcome. Similar to the earlier example, when you have someone else take photos to stimulate your imagination, you can obviously do the reverse. In the process of instigating an escape from ritualized thinking, you just might create a spark for yourself.

Clearly it would be fortuitous to have an endless amount of time for allowing our minds to wander. Most of us simply don't have that luxury. It's a comfort to know that our esoteric thoughts are an ongoing and subconscious process. It's usually a prudent choice to put a time limit on when we hope to reach certain answers. Creating an artificial timetable can accelerate even our most extraneous thinking, just as a task will take the time allotted.

Because we are accustomed to a world that is increasingly incessant about immediate responses, we can also practice using our imagination the same way. One example is to jot down a topic on the top of a page and then for the next ten minutes... write down as many ideas as you possibly can, even if they veer away from your focus. Remember to glance at the top of your paper on occasion, but the key rule is to not stop writing. If your mind goes blank, just write any words that you find interesting or even try drawing pictures that help you stay on track.

Another example is to convince ourselves that we absolutely must come up with a viable solution to a problem, good or bad, within sixty seconds. When the time is up, we must write "something" down... the best answer we have. By electing another topic and repeating this again, we'll build practice for when our real time factor is much more crucial..

Goals are dreams with deadlines.

A more effective way to implement the same strategy is to mimic the lesson from Socrates on wanting to breathe. Just by holding our breath until we have "some form" of a solution will conveniently force us into a limited time allotment. When we can lock into that same type of passion, and do it repeatedly, the result will be a larger number of answers to choose from, increasing the possibility for a phenomenal idea.

CHAPTER NINE

CHANGE YOUR LOOK

Book Sense

All the earlier exercises can be fun and entertaining, but they can also be wasted effort if they are not purposeful. Eventually we need to transform our new discoveries into some form of action. While we want our eyes to continually wander and explore, possibilities alone are barely measurable. In order to grow we need more than ideas, we have to make them real. So how do we condition ourselves to go from not only perceiving more, but to actually achieving more?

There's a time-honored story of a young boy who was eager to see the traveling circus when it came to a nearby town. Upon arriving before the main show, he noticed a huge elephant standing outside the circus tent. What made this moment so unusual and memorable for the child was while the elephant had a collar around one of its legs, it wasn't tethered to anything. The boy was quite bewildered and approached one of the workers to ask, "Isn't it dangerous for that elephant not to have a leash? Couldn't he walk all over the tent and smash it, or run through the town and scare everybody?"

The worker smiled and confidently replied, "As an infant this elephant was chained to a stake for the first few years of its life. He learned that he could never walk more than five feet from where he was tied. Since that feeling has been stuck in his memory for such a long time, we never have to chain him anymore. As long as he can feel his collar, he just assumes that he can never walk more than five feet from where we place him."

Tentative efforts lead to tentative outcomes.

As adults we have a propensity to live our lives the same way. It's as if we're anchored by an invisible chain and are nervous about wandering too far or thinking too erratically beyond our safety haven. Most first time acting students taking an "improve" class find it difficult to step outside of their shell and allow the world to see what crazy expressions and emotions they've held captive inside. At the risk of embarrassment, they soon learn there's much more to gain than lose by ignoring what others may think.

It would be much easier if we could simply hide behind a mask, as if attending a themed costume party, so we could let our inner child escape. Reminding ourselves to view as many aspects of life through the eyes of a child is a tremendous start. However, there's a more important factor for not only sustaining our curiosity, but making our dreams more tangible.

Not long ago I met a most remarkable and fascinating elderly man near my hometown. He was visiting Pennsylvania while on business and through him I learned an interesting story about a boy who had endured a problematic childhood. Apparently the boy's father had experienced an ongoing dilemma of finding stable work, and the result was that his son was constantly forced to migrate from school to school.

Because his educational environment was continually interrupted, it made any traditional learning a laborious task for him. He decided he would ultimately be most content to take on the work of his father, who worked as a horse trainer at an endless number of stables, ranches, and farms. Like his father, he had been around horses his whole life but was infatuated with them even more. He began taking a special interest in their training and felt very much at home in every aspect of their care.

The first and only time he ever became engrossed and excited about a school assignment was when one of his teachers asked the class to write about their personal goals in life. For once he was able to share his innermost feelings of wanting to work around horses. But rather than work for someone else like his father, with the instability it can offer, he decided for this project he would become the owner of a ranch himself.

He imagined the massive responsibility associated with a large horse ranch, resting on over a hundred acres, in which dozens of hired ranch hands actually worked for him. He even drew an elaborate sketch for his school project describing the precise layout of the stables, the training areas for the horses, a number of extra corrals, the on-site lodging for all his employees, and even a nice home for himself. He imagined a home high upon a hill, where he could look out over his entire property. He put more enthusiasm and involvement into this project than anything he had ever done in his life.

When he finally completed his all-encompassing paper and turned it in to his teacher, he felt confident for the first time he had done his homework to the best of his ability. But several days later when the papers were returned with a grade, his paper displayed a large red F on it with a note that said, "See me after class."

The boy was speechless and heartbroken. After class he went to his teacher and said, "I've never put so much thought and effort into any homework my whole life. How could I receive such a terrible grade?" She then glared at him saying, "Monte, this dream of yours is ridiculous and too farfetched. Your family doesn't have the necessary income to help you buy a ranch, pay employees to train all of these horses, and maintain such an extensive project. This paper was supposed to be about something more realistic; something you could possibly achieve after you finish school. Now, why don't you go home and reconsider what you'd like to write about, and then I'll reconsider your grade," she continued. "Just make sure that it's about something more reasonable for you to accomplish when you're no longer a student."

Made to feel like his dreams had been destroyed, he went home very discouraged. When he approached his father for help about how to handle what happened in school that day, he became disappointed again. His father's only advice was that this was something he would have to decide for himself. He wanted his son to contemplate how he would respond to his teacher's remarks, knowing that his choice might affect his attitude in the future.

The young boy dwelled on his father's comment long into the night, until he fell asleep. The next morning he went back to school and returned the very same paper to his teacher saying, "You can keep the F. I'll keep my dream."

After hearing about this story, the visiting gentleman kindly invited me to come and see the work that he's been doing in Isidro, California. When I arrived at the address he had given me, I found myself standing in front of a large gate with a sign that read, "Flag Is Up Ranch." Traveling up the long driveway I soon learned I was encircled by a one hundred and fifty four-acre property.

It was an active horse ranch with many stables, corrals, training areas, and living quarters for the staff of seventy-five people. High on a hill overlooking the ranch was a beautiful home where the gentleman, Monty Roberts, still lives. Above his fireplace is a framed piece of paper which just happens to have a big red F on it.

Since that time Monty's teacher has brought many of her new students to visit her former student's home. She teaches quite differently now as she explains you should never let anyone steal your dreams. If you can simply imagine something... anything is possible.

What made the difference for Monty is not only did he have a dream, but he also put it in writing. He had even drawn a descriptive layout he could visualize from time to time. When we put our thoughts on paper and have a tangible means of constantly refreshing our memory, our dreams have a much stronger likelihood of becoming a reality. This is an incredibly powerful tool for encouraging us to take action.

Things only said are not worth the paper they are written on.

Most of our memory is very short term, lasting only ten to twenty seconds. When we look up a ten-digit phone number, or even a seven-digit one, it's fairly difficult to retain it much longer than twenty seconds without writing it down. By writing out our goals, the probability of them fully materializing increases tremendously. While many of us already practice the value in writing certain things down, we usually disregard this when it comes to our creative side.

Possibly the strongest advice I can share is to prioritize a moment for purchasing a "blank book" specifically designated for your own creative thinking. Even more important is to keep it available for scratching down any ideas you have, at whatever sporadic time they come to you.

Your immediate argument may be you can just use your PDA, or any other electronic gadget you carry with you anyway. Although I've found, without a doubt, this never has the same impact as a specific book that is solely designated for this purpose. There is something freer and more conducive to creativity when you're able to draw and write in any format you like. The only remaining consideration, which is equally important to the equation, is to browse through it from time to time to reflect on your previous thinking and allow your subconscious mind to "play" with your new ideas.

The strongest memory is weaker than the palest ink.

As mentioned at the beginning of this book, pictures and drawings provide the fastest means of communication. So, the more we can make use of these for us to peruse from time to time, the quicker we will be able to jog our memory. The more emphasis we place on our blank book, by increasing our number of entries, the greater our chance for improvement.

Often when we read something motivational and inspiring we lose track of it before we have a chance to apply it. When it comes to striving for success, sometimes we miss the big picture. Far too many people feel that it's almost sacrilegious to write in a book. By all means, please write all over this book, or highlight whatever strikes you as interesting, or if you really want to live on the edge... tear out a page if that's what it takes to help you achieve something new. O.K., so now it's no longer completely intact for loaning to your friend or referring to later. But, if the page goes on your desk or bathroom mirror to remind you of something important, the cost is a fraction of what you would pay for a class or to hire a coach to accomplish the same thing.

Whether writing in this book or a blank book, an exciting aspect, which can't be appreciated until we've actually tried it first hand, is that all our efforts will continue to build momentum the longer we stick with them. If you've ever tried to push a car that won't start, even with several other people, you know how difficult it is to make it budge. But once the car's already in motion, it's much easier to keep it going. Even our bodies require an initial build up of adrenaline to meet some of our physical and emotional challenges. Taking advantage of this power of momentum allows us to develop ideas more quickly once we've started the process.

I experienced a lasting lesson in momentum during a trip to Mont Tremblant, Canada when our visiting ski club was offered five days of free lessons with our travel package. Since my friends and I were all about speed at the time, we signed up for racing lessons with Bobby Pond, a former medalist in the Olympics.

All week long, we were taught how to increase our speed as we traversed through the gates (the flags which designate a turn) using new mechanics that lessened our friction against the snow. We adjusted our approach into every turn and took advantage of aerodynamic ways to tuck our bodies, trying to knock off fractions of a second from each of our runs. Bobby provided many helpful guidelines for improving a variety of techniques essential for racing. Throughout the entire week, he and I had fun taking personal jabs at each other, all in good spirit. On the final day of class, while competing against all the other visiting teams, Bobby challenged me to one final race, even giving me a five-gate head start.

I immediately decided that even beyond all the new skills I had learned, I would risk falling in order to ski faster than I had ever gone in my life. Straightforward physics dictated to me that the fastest way to the bottom was to keep my tips pointed downhill while letting gravity do the rest. I was committed to not slowing down at any cost.

When the time came, I burst out of the starting gate and tried to accelerate every chance I could, using the steepness of the slope to its full advantage. I was determined not to let Bobby win this race, short of falling (which I could justify as a great excuse for losing). Before I was even halfway through the course, a giant blur rocketed past me as if I was almost standing still, and he only continued to gather speed the further he went.

How could that guy possibly propel himself so much faster than me when I already felt as though I was traveling at Mach Ten speed? As a professional athlete and an expert in momentum, he knew how to build upon all the techniques he had shared with us all week and combine them into world-class form that would work for him syner-gistically. Comparing myself to him, I felt as though I had made very little progress until I looked at my time trials over the course of the past week.

It's easy to become disillusioned as to how much progress we are making or how close we are to reaching a goal because of an incon-sistent point of reference. If you look at the two gray squares below, one appears to be much darker than the other. In reality, their colors are absolutely identical. It's just that our eyes are comparing them to the relative density of the colors adjacent to them, and our perception becomes distorted. By bending the page so the two gray squares are side by side you can prove this to yourself.

Most of our growth comes in tiny increments which almost seem invisible. Countless unseen details are usually the difference between mediocre and magnificent. While you and I may never reach the speed of an Olympic skier, we can use his understanding of momentum to increase the pace at which we improve. All we need is a conscientious effort to stay curious, a commitment to recording our ideas, and a periodic interest in referring to them... to keep us on the right page.

Unlikely Pair

With very few exceptions, we still have the same periodic chart in chemistry that we did centuries ago. Everything on the planet is comprised of one or more of these elements. The only difference is in how they are combined. Man has even been able to create new metals by restructuring what nature has already provided.

Understanding chemistry is essentially a study of the breakdown of components. First we must be aware of what we have to work with, and then we can compare one thing to another. From that we can study the infinite number of ways these components can be constructed to create everything we know.

The foundation of creating or inventing something new usually has its roots in combining two well-recognized ideas in an unlikely pairing. Ironically, they are often two items we either use or see frequently, but never associate with each other. The challenge is to become more aware of them, and then look for ways to compare them.

Randall Wise, a graduate from Harvard University, at one point came up with the idea of contact lenses for chickens. At first this sounds absurd. Who cares about how well chickens can see? But this unlikely pairing has another intention. When chickens are confined to an area too small, they have a tendency to peck at each other until the weaker ones die. This person's goal was to find a way to house more chickens within a smaller space without them killing each other.

He put red tinted contact lenses into the chicken's eyes that not only distorted their vision, but modified their behavior as well. The chickens still had a natural tendency to peck for feeding themselves, but could no longer see blood on the other birds which lessened their instincts to attack them. At a cost of about fifteen cents per pair of lenses, it proved to be a very frugal way of increasing the size of a flock without increasing the overhead (...poor chickens).

Often we are looking for something so new and unusual we miss a great idea found in the ordinary. How many times have you read about a new product and said, "Oh, that's so simple, why didn't I think of it?" Usually the idea has been sitting right in front of us, just waiting for someone to grab it. Yet somehow... it's imperceptible. We just don't see it. Or, better still, we may see it but just don't recognize it.

Approximately thirty years ago, there was a young boy from Russia who had taken a disastrous fall and broken his glasses. While being escorted to his eye doctor the boy barely realized he was not wearing his glasses because he was still able to see.

This seemed quite peculiar to Dr. Fyodorov because the boy's vision had always been poor. When he was examined closely, it was discovered that shards of glass from the lenses had just happened to graze his corneas in a way that partially corrected his sight. The doctor concluded that if this was even possible he should explore the concept of doing the same thing intentionally, which was the forerunner of radial keratotomy. This is a procedure wherein radial incisions are made in the periphery of the cornea with the intention of changing its curvature due to the pressure that is created by the fluid behind it.

These tiny cuts are made like spokes on a wheel through the majority of the corneal thickness to enhance a patient's acuity.

The result was effective, although it predisposed patients to an array of complications. As the technique progressed and was ultimately refined, it paved the way to most of the current techniques being used with Lasik surgery.

Often our greatest opportunities for growth are hidden within the depths of our challenges. The unlikely pairing of circumstances all around us can be used either intentionally or accidentally to awaken the way we think.

Everyone has an idea that could change the world. —Albert Einstein

---

Using the concept of "aware and compare," how do we go about keeping ideas fresh all day long in the midst of our mundane routines? It certainly helps to have something at our fingertips that will remind us of the many opportunities for unusual pairing. One method is to program our cell phones or PDAs to jog our memory.

Another easier and more effective way is to simply carry a few index cards cut in half to write down any words, thoughts, or objects that happen to catch your eye. Try not to make them too complicated. You don't need particularly unusual objects, as most ideas are found in the ordinary. You could notice a chocolate candy wrapper and decide to write down "foil." Or maybe you're adjusting a cat collar and decide to write down "Velcro" on the next card. Your words could vary from a lady's stocking to a silicon chip, the wing of a fly to a garden hose, or anything that holds the least bit of interest to you. Absolutely any word will work. There are no rules.

After you've collected a couple dozen words, blindly select just a few of them to carry with you. Once or twice during the day, choose two of the cards and think about any possible ways that they could coexist. Take advantage of the few moments you may have at a stoplight, or while waiting for someone to meet you. Be open-minded with an eye on your immediate environment (such as a word on a sign) for something to cause the spark that may tie your chosen words together. It may be something that initially even seems contradictory.

During my travels to Africa, a small native bird known as the Egyptian Plover intrigued me. If you are fortunate enough to follow one to its favorite food source, you may come face to face with a sizeable crocodile. This frail bird can often be seen picking the carnivorous remains from a crocodile's teeth after its full course meal. Obviously this huge reptile would have the luxury of an additional snack in the blink of an eye by merely closing its jaws on this feathered fellow, but it seems that the two share a symbiotic relationship. By living in this unusual harmony, the crocodile enjoys a free hygienist while the small bird has a free lunch.

Even nature has a way of unveiling extraordinary bedfellows to us on occasion. They are just another example of how some of the least likely candidates might compliment each other. Being open-minded to the unfamiliar can also give us unfamiliar answers.

You can read about the concept of pairing the words above, smile, and agree that it has some merit. Until you actually attempt it yourself, you will never truly appreciate its inconspicuous value.

Four Eyes

As mentioned earlier, having a few trusted friends as part of your personal brainstorming team can go a long way in broadening the way we think. Rather than miss the obvious, four eyes are better than just two. For an even better perspective, don't be too quick to settle for people that are close to you, as they may not be as candid or may share a viewpoint that's too similar to yours. It might be more helpful to share ideas with an acquaintance that doesn't know you well. In fact, the less they know about you and the further away from your field of knowledge, the better.

An opportune way to invent a better washing machine may be to speak with a twelve-year-old who's never even done laundry. The youngster may inquire about things that wouldn't typically come to mind. Why does the clothing have to get wet? Why can't you use steam instead of water? Why does the machine have to be made in this shape? Why won't it dry everything, too? They may ask all of the "why" questions we are quick to make assumptions about.

James Dyson was an artist, yet he developed the most popular household cleaning device of our time. The Wright Brothers were bicycle repairmen and didn't know enough about physics to realize (to their advantage) a heavy piece of metal can't fly through the air. Someone far outside our area of expertise will perhaps see the big picture easier from another perspective than we can and not be constrained by preemptive thinking.

It's vital not to forget that many great ideas are found where we least expect them. The single spot below seems to steal our attention more than the others, as though it is somehow more important. All the rest are clustered together as though they belong in the same category. But since every spot is the same, it's much easier to overlook some of the ones in the larger grouping. Don't miss the chance to find value deep within the ordinary.

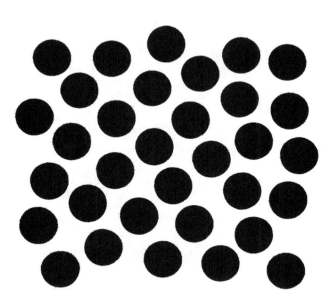

The less someone knows about us the more likely they might be to approach an idea from the exact opposite direction we would. This is similar to the reverse thinking mentioned before that illusionists use to solve a problem, first deciding what they want to accomplish, and afterward how to do it. In the same way, try to genuinely imagine that in ten years from now you will have achieved all your goals. Now, how did you get there? I believe one of my greatest fears would be to watch a video near the end of my years that reveals everything my life could have been. Most elderly people admit they are much sorrier for what they didn't do than what they did do.

Try to imagine all the events and memories that could have been a part of your life had you prioritized your time and money differently. At the end of the tunnel, how we spent our money is not as consequential as how we spent our time. We can remember the details of our vacation three years ago, but not the details of what we did three weeks ago. The routines of life fade very rapidly in contrast to the moments we make significant. In fact, the majority of yesterday has already become a blur. So we need to stop... right now... just for a moment. It's imperative to contemplate how we truly want to spend our future before it ends up behind us.

If you knew for certain you wouldn't fail, how would you live your life differently?

A fellow student at Penn State was an architect major, and he explained an exercise to me that was given by one of his professors. The goal was to not have students get locked into traditional thinking when trying to design something new. One day the instructor led the class into a carpeted area with no seating available. He advised everyone this was about to be a lengthy class devoted to drawing and they should make themselves comfortable on the floor while he left the room for a moment.

Upon returning three minutes later, the students had sprawled out all over the floor in a variety of positions. Some were resting on an elbow while others sat up straight. Still others leaned against the wall, while some lay flat on their stomachs. The professor looked down at the class and said, "Nobody move. For the next hour I want you to remain in the exact same position you're in at the moment and design a chair or sofa that would physically support you. Think of all the possible ways you could design a piece of furniture, using any materials or fabrics available, and then allow your imagination to wander."

If the professor had taken the class to the room, had them all sit in conventional chairs, and then asked them to draw a new chair design, he probably would have received many similar and commonly seen sketches. It's always possible to make small incremental improvements by tweaking what we already know. Sometimes these minuscule changes can be very valuable. However, if we want the prospect of making huge strides all at once, it helps to begin from an entirely new reference point.

There should be an extended round of applause for the Cincinnati high school teacher who instructed one of his classes to find an abandoned shopping cart and transform it into a motorized go cart. The students were expected to modify its size, develop a safe steering mechanism, and add a battery-operated motor that was perfectly functional. And yes, they were graded on it accordingly. It should be no surprise some of his students are now excelling as engineers in the real world.

I recall watching film clips from the early days of our space program, especially as the astronauts prepared to land on the moon for the very first time. In tandem there would also be several documentary-type broadcasts in an effort to share a glimpse of the astronauts' personal lives.

During several of these moments, you could witness them as they left their families carrying a suitcase to begin their extensive training at NASA. Isn't it intriguing that we had the technology to take a manned spacecraft all the way to the moon before we discovered we could put wheels on a suitcase? Time and time again our eyes fail to see what should be self-evident.

Winston Churchill once said, "If you can't say what you need to on one page, you don't know your subject well enough." In the same light, my favorite television commercials are usually the ones that are effortlessly simple, yet deeply profound.

As an example, I remember a Volkswagen commercial from long ago. The camera panned across a paralyzing snow blizzard that had nailed a suburban neighborhood of Middle America. Everything was completely covered in white which created an ominous, almost surreal setting. All you could see were the softly curved silhouettes of houses which more closely resembled igloos and a landscape that looked like an ocean of white powder.

Suddenly in the middle of the picture a garage door opened as a Volkswagen Beetle backed out onto the street and took off down the road despite the height of the freshly fallen snow. The camera shot watched the car disappear into the distance, as a single caption appeared which read, "Did you ever wonder how the man in the snowplow -- gets to the snowplow?" Simple... yet powerfully effective.

Another one of my more recent favorites I also felt was extremely effective only lasted ten seconds. The NFL sponsored it during a Super Bowl game after the halftime entertainment. The only thing it was

THE OTHER SIDE OF VISION

comprised of was its own NFL logo with a small caption underneath that read, "Thirty minutes from now, all the teams will be tied for first place."

What a motivating perspective and tactful way to create a premature incentive for the many fans not watching their favorite teams that day. While a particular team may not be playing in the Super Bowl this year, their next opportunity is right around the corner. Compare that to the hilarious and high energy commercials that are all too common to us. They may do a good job of making us laugh, but usually cost a fortune to produce and most people can't even remember who sponsored them. Changing our perspective may not only be more cost effective, but equally more influential.

Genius is often the ability to recognize the obvious.

There are certain parts of Disney World that are painted *every* single night because they're touched by so many thousands of hands all day long. Disney pays attention to such detail to make sure these sought out areas of the park look brand new the very next day.

Since many visitors are there for the first time (or were so impressed they came back again), Disney undeniably feels this first impression makes a monumental difference in how their entire venue is perceived. Time has proven they are right. It can be all too easy to take certain details for granted, especially the ones that really count.

Try not to overlook an opportunity to stand out among your peers because you missed seeing the obvious, the ordinary, or the invisible.

Take advantage of someone else's eyes (even the person you suspect to be the least likely to know) in being able to see what may be far too common for you to notice. Who can you think of that could offer you a fresh perspective of what you're missing?

Vocal Vision

In trying to implement concepts like aware and compare, reverse thinking, and looking for the invisible, how can we begin to modify our previous habits in hopes of immediate improvement? A proven physical change we can make which will instantly improve the way we emotionally and mentally see things is to simply change our vocabulary. Our vocabulary can, by far, be one of the most positive influences on our attitude and behavior.

I have many older patients that are apprehensive and confused about the possibilities of getting cataracts, glaucoma, or macular degeneration because of their family history. They can be fearful and overly anxious about the likelihood of becoming inflicted with the same forms of blindness other family members have suffered. By choosing my words very carefully, though, I can explain these ocular changes in a way that not only makes it easy for them to understand, but places their concerns in a truer context with the seriousness of a disease and newest technology available to help them.

As an example, when patients overreact to cataracts, I explain they're simply part of a natural aging process comparable to teeth turning yellow or hair turning gray. In other words, they are not a skin or a growth, and, if we live long enough, the change will probably happen to most of us. Since Medicare will pay for the majority of the surgery and because the visual improvement is comparable to that of Lasik surgery, I now know older patients who are actually praying for their cataracts to get worse so they can function without glasses. Suddenly I have completely changed their perspective, and they leave smiling rather than depressed.

We can't ignore that the tone of voice, the level of confidence, and the amount of sincerity with which we say something makes a decided difference as well. Most of what matters is our specific choice of words. Rather than saying, "I wonder if this is possible?" try, "Let's find the best way to accomplish this." Or, "What's the easiest way to make this happen?" Instead of referring to something as being "frustrating," replace that word with "challenging," or "a real learning process," or "requiring all of our resources."

Don't allow most things to overwhelm you. Think in terms of "rising to the occasion," or the determination that "no one can make you stumble" over such a trivial entity, or "this will never compare" to some of the outlandish situations you had to endure in the past. Rather than remind yourself of the few disrespectful people you have to deal with in a given situation, turn these people into "adventurous lessons in human behavior," or a "reminder gift" that all people are not like them. Sometimes we find that killing people with kindness is the ultimate revenge.

Remember, every mistake we've ever made is simply a valuable lesson in disguise. The key is to never refer to them as mistakes! Mentally, and even more so, "verbally," reference them as learning experiences. Each one of these landmark lessons takes us closer to our goals if we learn from them and are willing to see things from a new perspective.

> **The trials we encounter will introduce us to our strengths.**

The majority of businesses deal with customers... whether they are live or somewhere in cyberspace. The easiest way to grow these businesses is to turn these customers into *clients*. A customer is someone that you sell something to. A client is someone that you share something with. You advise them, you stay in touch with them, and you care about your long-term relationship with each other. It's all a matter of incremental degrees in the way we see someone.

Again, take Disney's example. At Disney World they don't have customers; they have *guests*. The word guest reminds me more of a friend that has been invited to share in something special, which is how Disney wants someone to feel. So, they begin the process very effectively with their vocabulary.

Also, rather than employees they have cast members. They are all aware that Disney's success depends upon a group effort, and they always maintain a team concept. Because we live in an entertainment economy, it sets the stage for the right mindset even if the "cast member" is just a vendor selling tee-shirts.

What we often fail to remember is a business or company has nothing to do with a multitude of desks or office machines taking up space in a particular building. It has little to do with any physical aspect at all. A progressive business in its most basic form can be reduced to a group of people with the same shared beliefs. So the vocabulary we select to use is vitally important for representing the business culture we want to reflect.

We can change our world just by being more selective with our words. By incorporating a positive vocabulary, we can greatly shorten the time expectancy for our success. If we continue to embrace that "tonight's the night," someday we'll be right.

You are successful the moment you start moving toward a worthwhile goal.

The most difficult part is in taking the first step, whether you're beginning a ten mile run or searching for an unusual way to solve a problem. The more we grin and are willing to take a light-hearted approach, the easier the answers will come. The people who own the best frame of mind will laugh their way to success.

I remember hearing of a class about relationships being taught at a nearby community college. One night the instructor asked the class how often they spent intimate time with their spouses. When asked if they did more than once a week, several people raised their hand. When asked about several times a month many more of the class raised their hand. Finally when asked at least once every couple months almost everyone held a hand up. The instructor then asked if she had missed anyone.

With all the excitement and eagerness of someone who had just won a million dollars, one little man in the back of the room started waving his hand frantically as he bounced up and down with a smile he couldn't contain. The whole class turned to look as the instructor asked him how often he spent intimate time with his spouse.

The gentleman screamed out, "Once a year!"

Quite confused, the instructor continued, "Well, that's certainly much less than average. Why are you so ecstatic to tell us that it's only once a year?"

Grinning uncontrollably, the man yelled out, "Because tonight's the night... tonight's the night!"

Some of the best laughs are undoubtedly the ones that sneak up on us out of nowhere. I remember having a large plant I had just purchased resting on the car seat next to me as I approached a drive-in bank teller. Attempting to offer a lighthearted comment, she quizzed, "Do you realize you have a plant sitting next to you?"

I replied, "Yes, I know. Some people like to talk to their plants, and others like to play music for them. I find my plants like it best when I take them for a ride." I tried to keep a straight face as she looked at me and swallowed her laughter for fear I was serious. Within a few seconds she laughed so loud everyone in the bank made her repeat our exchange of words several times.

Looking for the fun and comedic moments in life goes a long way into making the steps of any project more palatable. Not only will it speed the flow of new ideas, but it will also allow the power of momentum we discussed to gain traction more quickly.

While infants will typically laugh or giggle up to three hundred times a day, by the time any of us reach adulthood we are lucky to laugh or chuckle even twenty times a day on average. Even more disappointing is that our amount of daily laughter continues to decline with each decade. Sure, infants cry more than we do, too, but in comparison they are happier for much more of their daily existence, even though we can control our lives more than they can. We have the ability to change our perspective at any given moment, and yet more often we choose not to.

Laughter, and our ability to smile in the face of a challenge, is very representative of our vocabulary and overall disposition. While it's imperative to take certain aspects of life very seriously, we should never take *ourselves* too seriously. Sure, I need to treat a patient's questions about their health in a very understanding manner. I discuss each of their concerns cautiously and with the utmost respect. But I can also be thoughtful and encouraging in a humorously positive way whenever the opportunity presents itself.

We need more room to breathe within our meticulous routines and the trivialities of what we may think are the seriousness of life. There is always a lighter side within the grand scheme of things. Humor has its place in more aspects of our lives than we recognize. It has an especially huge impact on a positive vocabulary. The quicker we are to laugh, the faster our internal chemistry will physically change and act as a natural catalyst for creativity and optimal imaginative thinking.

Whether it is second nature for us or it takes the least bit of effort, we should always be quick to laugh "effortlessly" and practice selecting words that reflect a positive outlook.

Maybe Tomorrow

Sometimes it's hard to understand the long term impact of the even slightest of considerate gestures. Possibly the best metaphor is in the understanding of compounded interest which reveals the virtue of starting a savings plan or retirement account early. By starting with a penny and doubling it everyday, it would take only a few weeks until you became a millionaire. The difference in growth potential is staggering just by committing to a strategy sooner.

To give this doubling factor even more perspective, consider the tale of a princess who fell in love with a peasant. Before knowing him very long, she was anxious to wed this unlikely addition to royalty. But her father would not approve of the marriage. After much begging, the father decided to offer her male friend a simple task to fulfill in exchange for his daughter's hand. If the worker was successful, he would be welcomed into the royal family. If not, he would agree to never speak with her again.

The father pointed to his chessboard and said on the first day, the peasant would have to place a single grain of rice on the first square. On the second day, he would have to place two grains of rice on the second square. On the third day, he would place four grains on the third one, then eight grains on the fourth one, sixteen on the fifth, and so on. This would be repeated until he reached the last square on the board when each square would have received twice the number of grains as the previous day.

Seeing the endless fields of rice out the window, the prince readily accepted, as this would seem to be a very simple chore with so much rice at his disposal. But the king was much the wiser and easily able to prevent the marriage to his daughter. Knowing there were sixty-four squares on a chessboard, and basing his challenge on a fundamental principle of mathematics, he knew there weren't enough grains of rice in the entire world to satisfy his request.

For the first time in history, the number of people on the planet has doubled in one lifetime. I can remember back to the age of five when visiting a friend's home and seeing an ant farm for the first time.

While I looked at nothing more than two thin sheets of plastic filled with sand, my friend dropped a half dozen ants between the closely held panes as we watched them begin to burrow tunnels in every direction. They traveled slowly from one end to the other in search of food, while attempting to create a more suitable environment for themselves. It wasn't long before the ants had begun to multiply and seemed to be working together as a colony. Rather than travel the whole way from one end to the other themselves, they appeared to have some sort of system with shared responsibilities for completing certain tasks. Needless to say we were quite intrigued.

It wasn't long before the ant farm was teaming with ants. They could no longer pass each other in many of the tunnels and could barely even move in others. They displayed a frenetic energy quite different from the leisurely activity seen when they were first introduced to their new home. Many apparently died from either being trapped or for lack of food. I thought back to our discussions in school about how our planet has a limited supply of certain resources and how dependent we will become on each other as the world population continues to grow.

We have many phenomenal tools at our disposal for improving our lives and enhancing our personal success. Altering our perspective and expanding the limits of our thinking can accomplish even more. But the ant farm, which could theoretically represent a microcosm of our world, can be an inspiration for the unequalled and humanitarian ways we can invest in our imagination.

The sooner we commit to improving the way we see, the more positively we can affect a larger picture than simply ourselves. As vital as it is to build on what we already know, it is even more critical to embrace what we don't yet have answers to. Artificial deadlines can also be very helpful for exploring a greater magnitude of our imagination.

Second Sight

There are many areas of our globe that are crowded or poverty-stricken beyond what most of us would consider normal living conditions. While it can be exhilarating when one of our long-sought-after ideas finally reaches fruition, it is even more rewarding when it can benefit the health and survival of many others. In the same way we can learn much from teaching, we can also learn much from giving, too.

> **The quickest way to enrich your life is to raise your standard of giving.**

Sure, there are agencies, government programs, and non-profit organizations that contribute widely to many of these causes, but they are comprised of people like ourselves who can be distracted or lose their point of reference from being too close to what they want to see.

To push my own awareness and challenge my own perspective, I initiated several travel experiences in conjunction with the World Vision Organization. Their primary focus is in providing food, clothing, and education to less fortunate children around the world. While in optometry school, even with my exorbitant school loans mounting by the day, I decided I could at least make a small contribution to a child who would never have the same opportunities I do. Each month

I sent a very small sum of money to a child living in the highlands of Kenya and was told my gesture was enough to provide handsomely for him due to the economics of their country. Every month I continued this practice, knowing by giving up one gourmet coffee here I was giving him food for a week over there, in a famished part of Africa.

Over time I stumbled across various articles warning about the many charitable contributions that never reach their destinations. It could be because of fraudulent business practices that release only a tiny percentage of what is initially promised. Or it could be the company has all the right intentions but the money is somehow intercepted in transit before ever reaching its designated recipient. So I justified my meager donation by accepting that even if the child only received half of what I sent it would still certainly be better than nothing.

After graduating from optometry school and having (supposedly) supported Timothy for several years, I became more inquisitive about whether or not he was actually receiving most of the support money I had been sending, and if it was really being used for its intended purpose. I convinced myself to take a bold step and travel to Kenya, unannounced to the World Vision agency, to satisfy my curiosity. Except for the name of his tiny village, I flew to Africa without having a clue where to find him.

When I arrived in Nairobi it took me the better part of a day until I eventually found someone who had actually heard of Timothy's little village on a distant hillside. I tried to explain how much I could use this person's help, because I didn't speak Swahili. He and his friend, fascinated by my story of searching for this boy, agreed to assist me on the two-hour journey to the region where Timothy lived. After hours of winding dirt roads in an old, dilapidated Jeep, we came to the village. It consisted of nothing more than a dozen unpainted concrete block buildings that were covered in a very piecemeal fashion with corrugated tin roofs.

We questioned most of the thirty or forty people who lived in these primitive "shops" asking if they knew of Timothy. Fortunately one of my two new acquaintances also understood their local language, too, as it was quite different from the traditional Swahili of Nairobi. Finally someone recognized his picture and pointed up to one of the nearby hills saying he lived up there with his family.

Again we took off in our Jeep and within another thirty minutes arrived at the tiniest of shacks. There we found Timothy, in the same torn sweater he wore in every picture I had of him over all those years. It was soon apparent he, his parents, and his fourteen siblings lived in the two-room hut that was no larger than my first dorm room at Penn State. All the children were wearing the same fabric, which surely meant all their clothes were cut and hand sewn from the same bulk of material.

I was excited to finally learn Timothy had been receiving about eighty-eight percent of the money I had sent (the balance was used for administrative services and promotional efforts, which is a relatively small amount for the size of World Vision's overhead). Most of it was allocated for food, a lesser amount for his education, and the smallest portion for community housing. My opportunity to spend time with his family, nearby friends, and teachers was enriching. Their only possessions were a cow, a goat, and a chicken, and the family tried to give me their chicken—a third of everything they owned—as a token of their appreciation and for coming to visit their son.

The very small pittance I had been giving meant more to the family than I ever knew. I returned home with one of the most dramatic changes in my perspective I had ever experienced. For the first time I began to understand what was meant by the saying:

The moment you try to give something away, it is already coming back to you.

What impressed me even more about World Vision, though, was my second experience with them. While visiting Bangkok as a tourist, I learned World Vision had a presence in the city so I decided to stop by their local office. They offered to show me some of the local projects they were working on; one of them was especially disheartening. Numerous young families were living in makeshift homes only two feet above one of the sewage collection areas for the city. The stench was overwhelming and, if you fell off one of the narrow suspended walkways, you were most certain to contract a host of diseases.

On the spot, I decided to begin supporting an infant I came upon who was vomiting uncontrollably. Little Duanpen was in dire need of medical support to keep her healthy in these atrocious living conditions. As before, I sent a small and much needed amount of money that would help to sustain her life. A couple years later a letter I received from the organization stunned me.

The letter commented that Duanpen's father was finally able to secure a respectable job and the family was now able to move away from their past horrific conditions. It went on to say they no longer needed my donations for her (Wait, did I read that right? What charity would ever advise someone your donation has already fulfilled its purpose?), but if I would like them to, they would find another destitute child worthy of my support. Needless to say this organization deserves a high score for their integrity.

Until we travel and immerse ourselves into the physical act of walking beside someone in their culture, we will have a difficult time truly comprehending another person's point of view. And when we do, we may likely find it easier than we ever expected to make a considerable difference for him or her with very little effort, by altering our awareness. In hindsight, I learned much about the creative process and exploring my own imagination just by helping Timothy. He has taught me more than I could ever teach him.

Some of my patients actually initiate conversations about how they might help other individuals with compromised vision. They will usually ask if their older glasses can be recycled, knowing there might be someone else that could still benefit from them. The Lion's Club International is a big advocate of assisting less fortunate people with their vision problems and is actively involved in the re-dispersing of unused eyewear. Most of us are accustomed to having the best visual acuity possible and wouldn't consider settling for anything less, but there are many countries that are more than grateful to accept previously used glasses. They treasure what we discard.

When I was invited to join a volunteer healthcare team of doctors traveling to Haiti, the Lion's Club was very supportive. They were instrumental in helping me gather retired glasses that might be useful to people in one of the poorest countries in the western hemisphere. I offered my time to do eye examinations for the local people of Pignon during my visit. It was frustrating knowing I couldn't offer them the same standard of care I could in the U.S. because there was no financial support for an optical lab to make the perfect prescriptions they required.

During the moments I wasn't seeing my own patients I was able to lend a hand to other physicians doing general surgery. The unsanitary conditions and inferior equipment made every procedure extremely dangerous, and occasionally patients were lost on the operating table that never would have died under more favorable circumstances.

The greatest hurdle was in finding clean water. The local inhabitants had to carry buckets of water almost three miles, as they had no sophisticated plumbing. Again, traveling went a long way towards changing my perspective. By comparison, it again required very minimal effort on my part to make a meaningful difference for others.

Vision is not seeing things as they are, but as they will become.

So how can we begin to make a difference, right here at home, without having to travel thousands of miles? When I witness someone in a parking lot returning a shopping cart that isn't theirs, or someone else picking up a piece of litter that would have otherwise gone unnoticed, these tiny and almost insignificant acts demonstrate a person's ability to think from a unique vantage point. This will undoubtedly seem too trivial to many, but this subtle practice is rooted in the same mindset that can spawn monumental differences as it's magnified.

Have you ever had a desperate stranger ask you for money and found yourself in a quandary? Is this person legitimately poor or should I just ignore this whole situation? Does this person really need food, or will what I give just be spent on drugs, booze, or cigarettes? I often carry a small business card case with me just for this purpose. On one side is a stack of McDonald's gift certificates; the other side contains business cards for a local mission that offers free food and lodging for people in need.

The gift certificates ensure that what I offer can only be spent on food, so occasionally the person will decline. This immediately warns me they may not have been as hungry as they implied and probably had other intentions for the money. However, it does create a somewhat accurate barometer for me. When they do accept my offer, I may then be more inclined to give them something extra or be more supportive in helping them to find shelter. A small offering to make a difference in just one person's life is significant.

I paid a small fortune to attend a graduate school that was considered one of the best for my field in the country. However, I experienced a deeper education about life when I volunteered to help with a project a couple miles away that was run by someone nearly half my age.

One evening during a local newscast, a brief human interest story highlighted the problem with the ever-growing population of homeless people on the streets of Philadelphia. That night a young boy who lived nearby in a modest neighborhood said to his father, "Dad, there's got to be a way we can help some of them. I have an extra blanket I don't use. Can't we take it to share with at least one of them?"

His parents discouraged him, explaining that there were government agencies that focus on these types of problems and the dangerous streets are no place for a young boy. But day after day, for more than a week, young Trevor persisted until his parents finally gave in and drove him to one of the most poverty-stricken areas of the inner city one night.

They instantly became less comfortable upon entering this dark and dingy section that supported many grubby and unkempt vagabonds living on the streets. His parents locked the car doors, fearing for their safety. Suddenly, and without warning, Trevor unlocked one of the doors and ran across the street with his blanket, offering it to a disheveled man who was curled up on the sidewalk. "Here, sir," Trevor insisted, "Here's a blanket for you. I hope this keeps you warm."

**You are God's answer
to somebody's prayer.**

Somewhat stunned the man eventually replied, "Thank you. You're an angel in disguise." Then Trevor ran back to the car and his angry parents, who warned him to never leave the car again without their permission.

While his parents were pleased with their son's thoughtful intentions, they were also anxious to leave the frightening neighborhood. They were comforted knowing they had satisfied little Trevor's request and could leave that atmosphere and never return, but the next night Trevor begged to go back. And, once more, his parents tried to discourage him, but Trevor only became more adamant. Before long it became a nightly ritual for the family to return and offer a complete stranger a small token of comfort. When Trevor ran out of things from his own family to give, he began collecting items from all of his neighbors. Ultimately some of them became more supportive in helping to collect supplies for Trevor's homeless friends.

As time went on, Trevor's parents developed a sense of pride in their son's self-motivated mission project. Eventually they purchased an old building in the inner city for use as temporary living quarters for the homeless. The sign above the front door read "Trevor's Place." From that point forward, the rest of the street began taking on an improved appearance, which did much to lift the level of hope for its transient inhabitants.

I met and worked with Trevor while I was studying for my doctorate. How ironic he taught me it was possible to make a difference without a college degree, and he was a much younger student than I was. Trevor's motto became, "I am only one, but I am one. I can't do everything, but I can do something." He made such a great impression through his perception of sharing with people less fortunate than himself that word of his outstanding goodwill spread throughout the country. Eventually his generosity would reach almost every ear in the country. Ronald Regan honored Trevor Ferrell with the same award that had been given to both Gandhi and Mother Teresa.

Today Trevor's Place, which continues to shelter a hundred and fifty homeless children and their mothers, has expanded to Freedom Village. This new area supports entire families, many of whom were former inhabitants of the original Trevor's Place. It's amazing how a shift in perception of someone so young can influence thousands of others... even five times his age.

We were purposely created incomplete in order to rely on each other.

A small gesture that can't possibly be repaid can be more gratifying than if we expect something in return. While studying in Philadelphia I wasn't far from a hotel that was home to an exemplary employee. Working as a night manager he was an influential reason for much of the property's repeat business.

Late one evening an exhausted man and wife came in out of the rain on a stormy night hoping to find a room without a reservation. The hotel was completely full and the manager advised them they would need to look elsewhere. But seeing their disappointment and frustration, he decided to give up his own personal sleeping quarters just for that evening. At least he wouldn't be sending them back out into the horrible weather at such a late hour. And, because he wasn't able to offer them a standard room he didn't even charge them for their stay the next morning, hoping they would appreciate his hospitality and possibly return someday.

His sincere efforts in accommodating them so unselfishly undoubtedly made a lasting impression. Years later, that same gentlemen who had occupied the manager's own personal quarters for the night, called him with an intriguing invitation. To offer his appreciation for his memorable night's stay he stated, "You're the kind of person I would like to have in *my* hotel. Would you please take the time to come and visit me in New York City?"

He advanced the manager the necessary train fare for traveling to his own business for an interview. When the manager, George Boldt, arrived at the street address given to him by the man on the phone, he found himself standing in front of the Waldorf Astoria. He was given a job at one of the most prestigious hotels in the city, just by virtue of having altered his perception in the moment... to help a total stranger.

Sometimes a reward for doing the right thing may sneak up on us when we don't see it coming. But an honest goodwill gesture is done without expectations. We can never plan or foresee the potential outcome for even the smallest attempts to help someone. But that's part of the wonderful mystery of life and the quintessential reason for changing our perspectives and exploring our imagination.

CHAPTER TEN

INNOVISION

O ne of our definitive gifts is the ability to dream, and one of our second greatest is the ability to rationalize. We can either turn our goals into reality, or forever substantiate our circumstances and why we never accomplish more than we do. The thought process for staying positive and focused generally takes less time and energy than it does to justify reasons why we should just stop trying; it is merely a choice.

A guaranteed way to achieve more is to perceive more. Improving your perception is not about searching for solutions as much as maintaining awareness for new ways of seeing and discerning. Rather than thinking in terms of reality it requires openness to endless possibilities.

The recipe for a basic platform that encourages us to succeed more, enjoy more, and give more can be outlined as follows: Constantly search for new ideas; be relentlessly curious. Write down all your thoughts and review them on occasion. Take some form of action; make an attempt at anything. And finally, modify your game plan based on what you learned.

And, obviously the more often we repeat these steps the quicker we'll get results. There are no hidden secrets or shortcuts among creative people. The ideas don't drop out of their heads like magic. They are simply more accustomed to following the protocol above. As it is often heard, "there's no elevator to success... you have to take the stairs."

Remember that we can never be too curious, even about the most obvious and mundane aspects of our lives. Try to break the train of everyday thought, and never let worry be a substitute for action. Always try to look at things from an angle that may have never been explored before... the more options, the better. We frequently hear that "every great success was once considered impossible," so challenge all of your assumptions. Assume you have already achieved your goal, then decide how you did it. And whenever that light bulb goes on be sure to record your thoughts, as fifteen seconds later they may be lost forever. Then, even before you're ready, do "something," any form of action, to keep from squandering the precious time you'll waste by going into your head too much. Don't be afraid to take a risk, especially if you stack most of the odds in your favor.

Life truly is a room full of windows, and we can either choose to look at the walls, or through the panes. Finding just one that offers new insight could rival a lifetime of education. Since it doesn't cost any more in time, money, or effort, we may as well dream as big as possible; we could be short-circuiting ourselves by wasting our time with smaller ones? Letting our minds travel as far as possible can be invaluable, as these irrational thoughts can be much more powerful than facts. In the process we may even come across a new and untapped resource... an unexplored territory of ourselves.

After new triggers have encouraged ideas to flow and you've renewed your childhood sense of curiosity, here is a viable game plan to elevate your success. First, choose a passion that's close to your heart.

Whether it is innate or has developed over time, try to make it a permanent and prominent extension of you. Then change your perspective of it in as many ways as possible. Think of it in terms of *your* perception versus reality.

Next, personalize it so that it bears your signature. Take advantage of all your thoughts and life experiences to shape it, since no one has had a voyage quite like yours. Finally, be inexhaustibly persistent. Remember the famous quote: "you can not possibly fail if you always try one more time."

The key words are: passion, perspective, personalize, and persistence. None of these require *much* effort, but they do require *consistent* effort. Since you are focusing on your passion, it shouldn't feel like work. Enjoy the excitement of your dreams, but don't jump ahead. The most important use of your time is to be present... right here ...in the moment.

There are two important days in every week that never deserve our unjustified worries and concerns. The first is yesterday, which represents a host of mistakes that can't be erased and are already part of history; the second is tomorrow, as we continually look ahead to what could go wrong rather than living in the moment. Maintaining our focus on what's in front of us *now*, today, is the only way we can recover from our past and actively shape our future. It's been said that "in just two days... tomorrow will be yesterday."

Finally, make a conscious effort to relax more often and be open to anything that presents itself. Take a deep breath and welcome the unique opportunity to live in *your* moment. Remain aware and compare whatever's in front of you, no matter how common it may seem. Be knowingly persistent, understanding the more you repeat this simple process the more likely one of your ideas will flourish. Each of these steps can be a fun process and a continuous source of entertainment when you adopt the right mindset.

Always be content with what you have, but never with who you are.

If I could create anything, it would be some type of device or instrument that would actually allow someone to sense and feel what it's like to see through another person's eyes. It's impossible to understand exactly what another individual is experiencing until the day a doctor tells us we, too, have the same terminal disease. Likewise, we will never comprehend another person's excitement or satisfaction until we've sat in the same roller coaster seat or endured the same lengthy training process (with equal amounts of perspiration, labored breathing, and increased heart rates).

Probably the most feasible way we can hope to mimic the same emotional and mental state of someone else is by traveling and genuinely attempting to see the world through a new set of eyes. Whether you're on a vacation, on your way to work, or walking to another room of your home, strive to take a slightly different path than you've always done in the past. The further away from your normal routine the better.

If before graduating high school every senior were required to donate three weeks of their time to a third-world country, I believe they would learn more in those few weeks than all the education they acquired during the previous three months. Their vision would expand not only from a new perspective for a worthwhile cause, but by submerging themselves into a completely foreign culture while discovering a deeper appreciation for others as well as the home they came from.

What a guaranteed way to open the floodgates for innovative thinking and allowing young peoples' imaginations to soar. Beyond that, envision the goodwill it would generate toward other countries and the likelihood some parts of the world might even change their perception of us.

As you try to incorporate some of these perceptual concepts into your own life, I'll continue working on allowing one person to truly experience the vision of another. If we both keep our eyes open, we are sure to make some unique discoveries along the way. Please remember that everything once considered impossible began with one person's interest in using their eyes differently. The way we use our vision can make all the difference, not only in what we see, but in where we find our purpose.

RECOMMENDED READING

The Art of Possibility: Transforming Professional and Personal Life
by Rosamund Stone Zander

The Next 100 Years: A Forecast for the 21st Century
by Thomas Friedman

Predictably Irrational: The Hidden Forces that Shape Our Decisions
by Dan Ariely

Magic in Theory: The Theoretical and Psychological Elements of Conjuring
by Peter Lamont and Richard Wiseman

Blink: The Power of Thinking Without Thinking
by Malcolm Gladwell

Influence: The Psychology of Persuasion
by Rober Cialdini

How Brains Think: Evolving Intelligence, Then and Now
by William H. Calvin

Virus of the Mind: The New Science of the Meme
by Richard Brodie

The Starbucks Experience: Turning Ordinary into Extraordinary
by Joseph Michelli, Ph.D.

Right-Sizing Your Life: Simplifying Your Surroundings
by C. J. Ware

Hope for the Flowers: A Tale Partly About Life, Mostly About Hope
by Trina Paulus

The Entertainment Economy: How Mega-Media Forces are Changing Our Lives
by Michael J. Wolf

Wake 'Em Up!: How to Use Humor & Other Professional Techniques to Create
Alarmingly Good Business Presentations
by Tom Antion

ACKNOWLEDGMENTS

Life is busy, and yet there are many individuals who we think of often because they have touched our lives in a way that we will never be the same... thank you.

In addition, my parents could not have been more supportive and trusting in allowing me to find my own path in life.

I am very fortunate that Joe Curcillo and Dave Knox are the kind of dependable friends everyone wishes they had over the years.

I'm also a better person for knowing David Starr as both a brainstorming and travel companion. And there's no one I've shared more dangerous and outrageous escapades with over the past twenty-five years than my good friend Rob Albergo.

And finally, my unparalleled inspiration, never-ending reason to smile, and favorite motivation for always wanting to be present and in the moment, are because of Nanette and Whitney.

To my readers, I say "Thank you, sincerely!" I have customized and crafted this book with a variety of interests in mind. I invite you to stay in touch with me. Let me know if this experience has altered *or* focused the way you "look" at the world around you.

As you may have noticed throughout these pages, I like to bring home my key points with memorable lines and quotations. Some of these quotations are my own, some of them are attributed to their origins, and some of them are Favorite Sayings I have admired or repeated to my audiences in my repertoire over the years. When it comes to quotable quotes, I am a devoted enthusiast. If "Imitation is the sincerest form of flattery" ...then, please consider me among your biggest fans if I'm repeating a quote from you.

For more information, please visit:

THEOTHERSIDEOFVISION.COM

DRJAYSTERLING.COM

IMAGICORP.COM

REFERENCES

Peter Carroll, O.D., PA College of Optometry, Physiological Optics, 1975

Alvin Byler, O.D. PA College of Optometry, Geometrical Optics, 1976

Lorraine Lombardi, O.D. PA College of Optometry, Ocular Neuroanatomy, 1975

Greta Crozier, O.D. PA College of Optometry, Ocular Anatomy, 1976

"Vision and Learning Disability" by the American Optometric Assoc., 1976

"20/20 is Not Enough" by Seiderman and Marcus, Ballantine Books, 1989

"Virus of the Mind" by Richard Brodie, Hay House, 1996

"Predictably Irrational" by Dan Ariely, HarperCollins, 2008

"Lateral Thinking" by Edward de Bono, Harper and Row, 1970

"The Entertainment Economy" by Michael J. Wolf, Random House, 1999

"Trevor's Place" by Frank and Janet Ferrell, Harper and Row, 1985

Alan Brown, Grove United Methodist Church, West Chester, PA, 1989

Thomas Fries, Hempfield United Methodist Church, Lancaster, PA, 2005

Erismann, T., and Kohler, I. (1953). *Upright vision through inverting spectacles* [Film]. University Park, Pennsylvania: PCR: Films and Video in the Behavioral Sciences.

Erismann, T., and Kohler, I. (1958). *Living in a reversed world* [Film]. University Park, Pennsylvania: PCR: Films and Video in the Behavioral Sciences.

www.nytimes.com/2008/04/15/science/15titanic.html, April 15, 2008

urbanlegends.about.com/od/music/a/violinist_metro.htm, January 6, 2009

money.cnn.com/2007/06/12/pf/vacation_days_worldwide/, June 13, 2007

www.cfcl.com/vlb/Cuute/f/quiz.txt

en.wikipedia.org/wiki/Motion_aftereffect

www.thecoca-colacompany.com/.../cokelore_newcoke.html

en.wikipedia.org/wiki/The_Decca_audition

en.wikipedia.org/wiki/James_Dyson

www.funagain.com/control/product/...id.../~affil=WGPX

www.supersecrets.com/discover_more/win_lottery

www.thetreeofliberty.com/vb/showthread.php?t=36754

www.ehow.com/about_5040727_history-fortune.html

www.forbes.com/.../marketing-advertising-jacktrout-cx_jt_1024trout.html

en.wikipedia.org/wiki/Tom Amberry

www.americanwaymag.com/so-woodland-bar-code-drexel-university

www.artfulgolfer.com/2007/11/artful-major.asp

www.centennialofflight.gov/essay/.../kittinger/DI29.htm

www.citypages.com/1996.../chronicles-of-the-self-published

www.auntieannes.com

en.wikipedia.org/wiki/Pareto_principle

en.wikipedia.org/wiki/Lost Boys of Sudan

en.wikipedia.org/wiki/Edward C.Banfield

en.wikipedia.org/wiki/Linus Pauling

en.wikipedia.org/wiki/Spider_silk

en.wikipedia.org/wiki/Human echolocation

www.inc.com/magazine/19890501/5636.html

en.wikipedia.org/wiki/Egyptian Plover

www.free-articles-zone.com/.../The%20History%20of%20LASIK

corporate.disney.go.com/careers/culture.html

www.thetalentjungle.com/alumni/modules.php?name

en.wikipedia.org/wiki/Roger_Shepard

en.wikipedia.org/wiki/Ponzo_illusion

www.scientificpsychic.com/graphics

en.wikipedia.org/wiki/Kanizsa_triangle

en.wikipedia.org/wiki/Ehrenstein_illusion

www.psychologie.tu-dresden.de/i1/.../depth_ambiguity.html

www.shapirolab.net/Illusions/Checker%20Board.html

INDEX

TreeNeutral™

Advantage Media Group is proud to be a part of the Tree Neutral™ program. Tree Neutral offsets the number of trees consumed in the production and printing of this book by taking proactive steps such as planting trees in direct proportion to the number of trees used to print books. To learn more about Tree Neutral, please visit **www. treeneutral.com**. To learn more about Advantage Media Group's commitment to being a responsible steward of the environment, please visit **www.advantagefamily.com/green**

The Other Side of Vision is available in bulk quantities at special discounts for corporate, institutional, and educational purposes. To learn more about the special programs Advantage Media Group offers, please visit **www.KaizenUniversity.com** or call 1.866.775.1696.

Advantage Media Group is a leading publisher of business, motivation, and self-help authors. Do you have a manuscript or book idea that you would like to have considered for publication? Please visit **www. amgbook.com**